Picasso
and Cubism

Kay Hyman

JG PRESS

DAWN OF MODERN ART

Picasso
and Cubism

Kay Hyman

Contents

3 Introduction
3 **Picasso** and Braque
30 Gris
37 Léger
41 Delaunay
43 Villon and Duchamp
47 Derain
49 Dufy
51 Herbin
52 Gleizes
53 Kupka
54 Le Fresnaye
56 Lhote
58 Le Fauconnier
59 Marcoussis
60 Metzinger
62 Picabia

Published in the USA 1994 by JG Press
Distributed by World Publications, Inc
JG Press is a trademark of World Publications, Inc
455 Somerset Avenue, North Dighton, MA 02764
ISBN 0-9640034-5-7
North American Rights only

The Dawn of Modern Art
is an imprint of Cromwell Editions Limited and Ninic & Ninic

Designed by Paul McTurk BA MCSD
Printed by Tiskarna Ljudske Pravice, Slovenia

Introduction

The term "Cubism," applied to a movement of fundamental significance not only in art but for all aspects of design in the twentieth century, originated at an exhibition, the Salon des Artistes Indèpendants, held in Paris in 1908. The artist Georges Braque entered seven canvases but withdrew them all when five were rejected by a jury including Henri Matisse, who referred to them as "entirely constructed of little cubes." The critic Vauxcelles wrote of the subsequently exhibited paintings, "Monsieur Braque despises form and reduces everything, landscapes and figures and houses, to geometric patterns, to cubes." Although adopted by Cubists themselves, the name Cubist is not, however, very helpful, and relevant only to the initial years of the movement, whose members went on to develop their own different styles.

Picasso and Braque

Picasso and Braque were the painters directly responsible for the birth of Cubism, but it also drew inspiration from the work of previous, Post-Impressionist artists, specifically Cézanne and Seurat, and, less directly, from van Gogh and Gauguin. Matisse headed a group known as the "Fauves" or "Wild Beasts," to which Braque briefly belonged, which was strongly influenced by van Gogh's and Gauguin's use of color. Fauvism and Cubism had much in common in their more extreme versions of Impressionism's revolt against inflexible, realistic academic art. Both movements promoted artistic liberation, but differently, Cubism pushing artistic boundaries further, so the two groups became opponents and rivals.

Seurat's scientific analysis of color interested the Cubists, but the predominant influence was Cézanne, with his "architectural" approach to nature: "Everything in nature is based on the sphere, cone, and cylinder. One must first learn to paint according to these simple shapes." Early Cubist painting followed Cézanne's forms, color and brush strokes to the extent that it is known as "Cézannesque Cubism," the firmest move in art away from representation and towards the abstract. Braque was the first to adopt Cézanne's abstraction, in landscape, from the natural to the geometrical, also borrowing Cézanne's restricted color range (ochres, siennas, blue-greens) and the construction, rather than just coloring, of forms with short, diagonal brush strokes, ie *Houses at L'Estaque* . Raoul Dufy's early landscapes, painted at the same location, are similarly influenced by Cézanne.

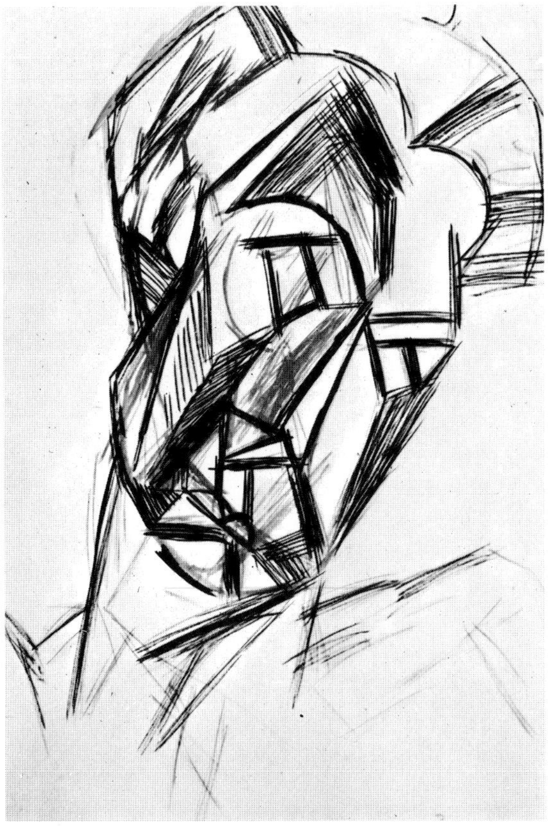

Picasso: *Head,* 1909

All the phases of Cubism, Analytical, Facet, Synthetic, Curvilinear etc, are reflected in the numerous, and dramatically changing, painting styles of Pablo Picasso (1881-1973).

Picasso was born in Malaga, Spain, the son of an artist and art teacher. After great success at art schools and immersion in Barcelona's avant-garde, he first went to Paris in 1900, settling there permanently in 1904 in a tenement studio in Montmartre known as the "bateau-lavoir" ("floating laundry"). His first show in Paris, in 1901, was not appreciated by the critics, who highlighted his debt to other artists, particularly Toulouse-Lautrec. Picasso, in fact, always borrowed, he has been dubbed a "master thief", saying himself, "I don't hesitate, if anyone shows me, for example, a collection of old drawings, to take from them anything I like." He did not, though, merely imitate, but fully incorporated the borrowed material into his own form of expression.

This was the time of his Blue and more formal Pink periods, both sentimental in tone. In 1906 Picasso abruptly turned his back on realistic artistic style and his work began to reveal two new sources of inspiration. The first, following a holiday in the Spanish Pyrenees, was sculpture of the pre-Roman Iberian and the Romanesque periods.

Picasso's portrait of Gertrude Stein was painted initially in the mode of his Pink period but, on returning from the Pyrenees, he repainted it in the Iberian style. The second influence was primitive African sculpture, introduced to Picasso by Matisse, an enthusiastic collector of such work. The Fauves valued it as an antidote to excessively civilised academic art but Picasso reacted on an esthetic level: African sculpture was essentially simple, yet lively, expressive and its design perfectly abstract.

This forceful change of artistic direction was expressed in *Les Demoiselles d'Avignon*, started in 1907 and left unfinished. The preparatory work for the painting traces his artistic development: the early sketches have more representational figures, which in the final version are rendered abstractly as basic human forms. Picasso described this distillation process: "In my case a picture is a sum of destructions." This picture is referred to as the first Cubist painting but it still owes much to Cézanne in feeling, while the arrangement and subject matter are reminiscent of Cézanne's *Grandes Baigneuses*. Nevertheless, the impact on Picasso of Iberian and of African sculpture is evident, though they are reflected in the painting in surprisingly separate ways. The Iberian influence has given the three figures on the left simplified faces with prominent eyes. The African contribution is to the two figures on the right, which, in stark contrast, are angular, their faces like primitive masks, with features distorted and parallel lines echoing the grooves of the sculptural source. Picasso had already painted the first set of figures in the Iberian style when he came across African sculpture, which imbues the other. *The Demoiselles*, though painted quite realistically, was the starting point of Cubism. From here evolved Analytical Cubism, developed later by Picasso and Braque, the breakdown or "analysis" of natural forms into seemingly random shapes and colors, until the representational element all but vanished.

Cézanne continued to influence the painting of Picasso and his followers for some years. Derain's *Martigues*, for example, draws on Cézanne's landscapes while using the bright colors of the Fauves (to which Derain had briefly belonged) in Gauguinesque flat patterns. In *Still Life on a Table*, Derain owes much to Cézanne, whose optical distortions he accentuates. André Derain (1880-1954) was profoundly influenced by Vlaminck, worked with Matisse, then, in the company of Picasso and Braque, became involved with Cubism without altogether accepting it. He later painted more realistically, incorporating a wide range of influences.

In 1908 Picasso was painting in various Cubist styles. *Dryad* is similar to *The Demoiselles* in that it is the simplified form of a nude woman. Picasso's later abstract works are heralded in *Woman with a Fan*, with its simple, flattened, angular forms. *Woman with Mandolin,* painted in the following year, features the "simple shapes of nature" that Cézanne had noted.

The dramatic impact of Facet Cubism then began to make itself felt. Rather than simplified, pictures became increasingly complex, with forms shattered into minute pieces and put together again as multi-faceted gems. Viewers need to remove themselves from the painting's representational aspects in order to concentrate on the visual "harmony" produced by all its other compositional elements. Representational painting, for example that of Cézanne, generates this kind of "harmony" as a side-effect, but it is central to abstract art. Not that Facet Cubism is entirely nonrepresentational: in Picasso's *Seated Woman*, Braque's *Violin and Palette*, and Picasso's *Portrait of Ambroise Vollard*, the subject matter is perfectly clear, to the extent that the portrait of Picasso's picture dealer is demonstrably accurate.

Any claims to realism had dissolved by the following year, 1911, when Picasso painted *The Accordionist* and *The Poet*. In the former painting the only discernible connection with its title is a set of keys at its centre; in the latter there are just allusions to a fine face with a mustache. At this time Cubism relied not so much on curves as straight lines, sometimes punctuated by a small circle or arc. The color selection was narrow: muted and harmonised browns, creams, grays, set off by black and white. These tendencies were in part the result of Cézanne's moderating influence, but also due to Cubist opposition to the Fauves, who favoured curvy, decorated, vividly colored paintings. The Cubists reacted with formal, structured asceticism.

Georges Braque (1882-1963) is usually regarded, with Picasso, as the cofounder of Cubism, though in fact it was Braque's pioneering work fragmenting landscapes in the style of Cézanne that provoked the movement's name. Braque and Picasso first met in 1907 at the "floating laundry." Braque's initial response to seeing *The Demoiselles* was acutely acerbic: he accused Picasso of serving "cotton rags washed down with turpentine." Immediately after, the two painters worked similarly but separately, coming together as partners in autumn 1909. Braque remarked, "We were like two climbers roped together on a mountain."

Their work is often similar, as they influenced each other profoundly, but their radically different personalities shine through their paintings. Picasso is extreme, temperamental and fiery; Braque is rational, contemplative and restrained. Their physical appearances mirrored this contrast. Picasso is generally regarded as the greater artist, in terms both of output and impact, but the quality of Braque's work can be higher in individual instances. Picasso is stronger, livelier, more vivid and emotional, but Braque's more even, harmonious and elegant painting can actually be more beautiful. Braque's orderly nature had made it impossible for him to continue as a supposedly riotous and chaotic Fauve: he commented, "You can't remain forever in a state of paroxysm."

Despite his less overtly "creative" approach, Braque was responsible for certain of Cubism's most original ideas. He began to introduce elements drawn from house decorating (these were familiar—his father was a house painter and decorator), like wallpaper, wood grain and marbling effects, and lettering, into his paintings, at first imitations and then the real thing.

Braque's *Valse* includes imitation wood graining and lettering. In a Cubist picture lettering is often merely decorative with no verbal meaning, though in this case there are connecting musical allusions: curving shapes and wood grain alluding to stringed instruments, a violin neck and sound-box hole, tuning keys. The lettering in *Still Life on a Table*, in contrast, is pure decoration. Picasso employs lettering differently in *The Aficionado*

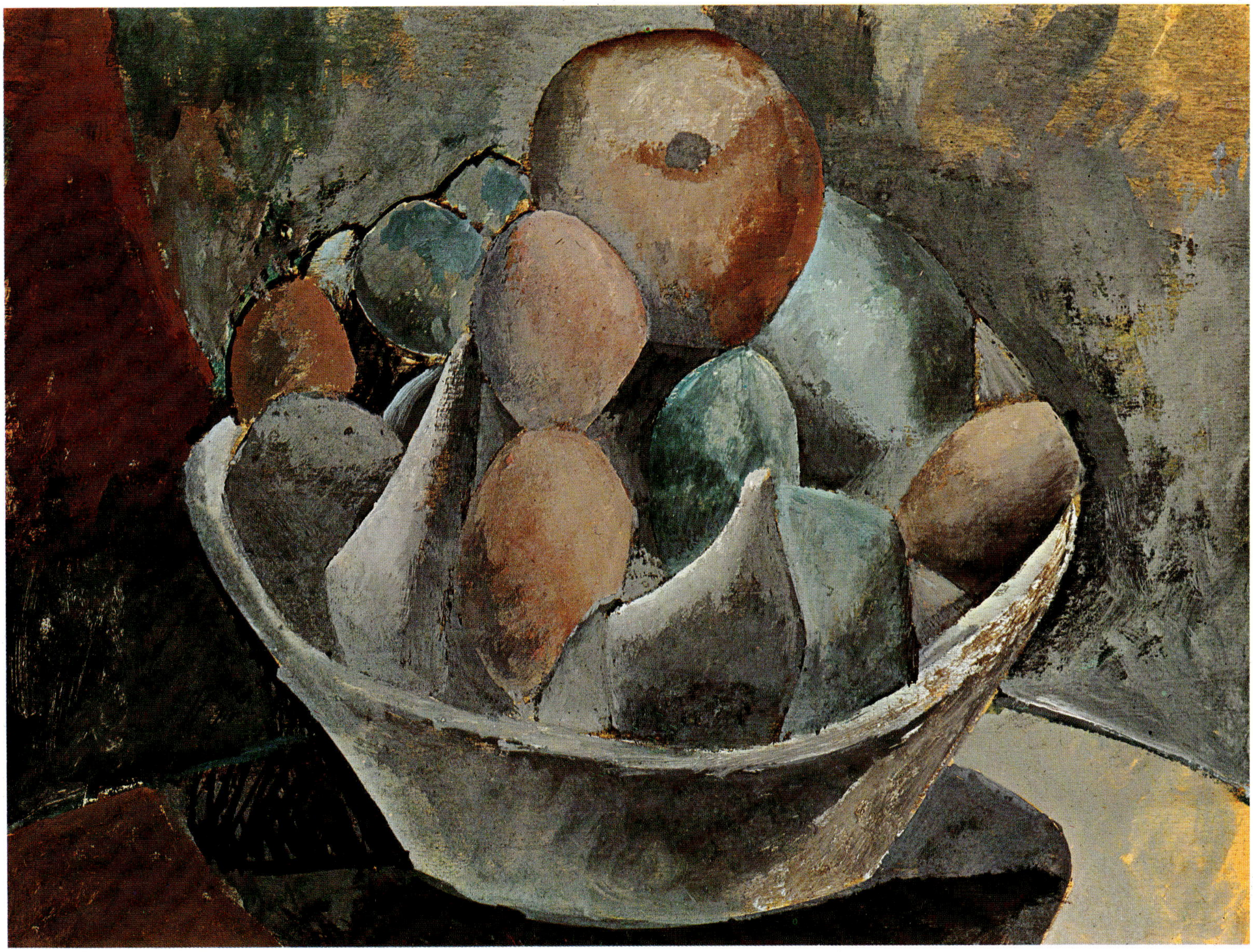

Pablo Picasso: *Fruit Bowl,* 1908

throwing light on what might otherwise be an obscure painting. "TOR", "Torero" and "Nîmes" (where there is a famous bullring) firmly establish the bullfighting context. One critic wrote, " Picasso and Braque incorporated in some of their pictures letters from labels and printed matter, because label, notice and advertisement play a very important role in the modern city, and are well-suited for inclusion in works of art."

Braque also introduced *trompe l'oeil* ("deceives the eye") in his paintings, depicting items so realistically that they invite touching, for example the nail at the top of *Violin and Palette.* This particular device has the twin effects of turning upside-down the usual arrangement of a still life and at the same time injecting unexpected and unexplained realism into the midst of total abstraction. The next move was obviously "collage": incorporating (literally, "gluing") an actual object into the picture. Picasso's *Still Life with Chair Caning* includes a real piece of oilcloth. Materials most often chosen for collage were wallpaper, newspaper, postage stamps, matchboxes, and rope, while Braque was known to mix sand into paint to enliven the texture. The relative realities of the objects and the paintings to which they were attached could be compared, while the fact that these everyday items should function in a work of art at all was a revolutionary idea in itself.

By now the Cubist movement had evolved yet again, into Synthetic Cubism. Analytical Cubism produced deconstructed versions of real things, but Synthetic Cubism used actual objects as sources of ideas for improvisation and further construction, leading to paintings with large, simple planes, forceful designs and textural emphasis. Picasso's *The Violin* is an instructive example, allusive and evocative of its violin motif, but neither directly representing it

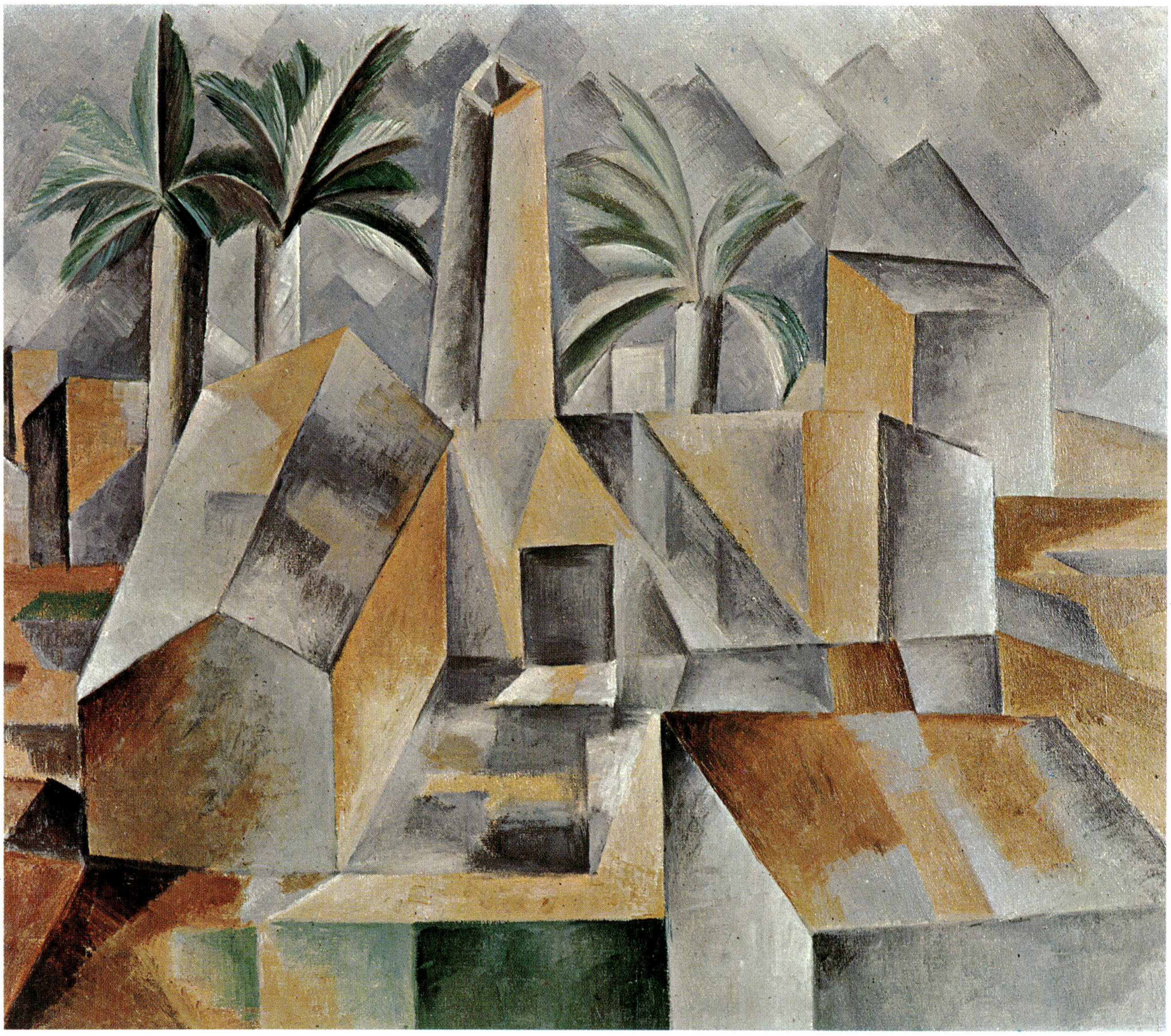

Pablo Picasso: *Factory at Horta de Ebro,* 1909

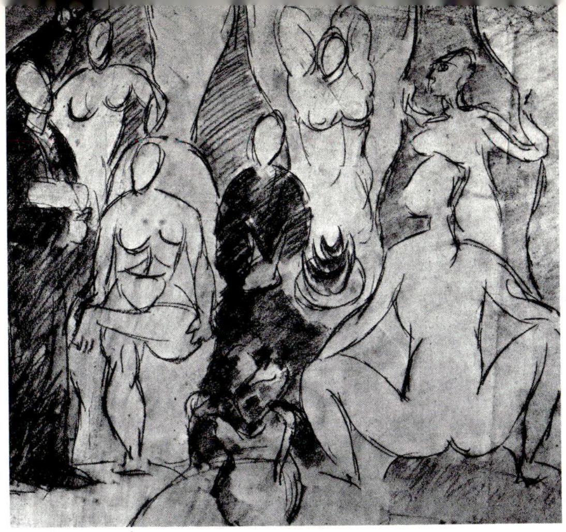

Picasso: *Study for Les Demoiselles d'Avignon*

nor attempting to break it down, to "analyse" it. The words "Jolie Eva" appearing in this painting (and others of the period) are there partly for decoration but also in reference to a new lover of Picasso's, Marcelle Humbert. Music is a recurrent theme in the works of Picasso and Braque, perhaps reflecting at some level the visual "harmony" of abstract art. Braque's *The Musician's Table* features multiple musical allusions: the curves of violins and guitars, sound-box holes, sheet music lines, and the beginning of the word "valse."

Both painters' abstract works became more curved in form and more richly varied in shade after World War I, for example Braque's elegant still lifes. Picasso, after being present at the birth of Surrealism, had a Neo-Romantic phase beginning in the mid-1920s. The two artists succeeded in extending their work beyond painting. Picasso designed stage sets for the ballet, illustrated books, and involved himself in lithography, sculpture and ceramics; at one stage he was director of the Prado in Madrid. Braque, similarly, was occupied with stage set design, book illustration, sculpture and graphic work; on contrasting scales, he designed stained-glass windows for a small church and decorated a ceiling in the Louvre.

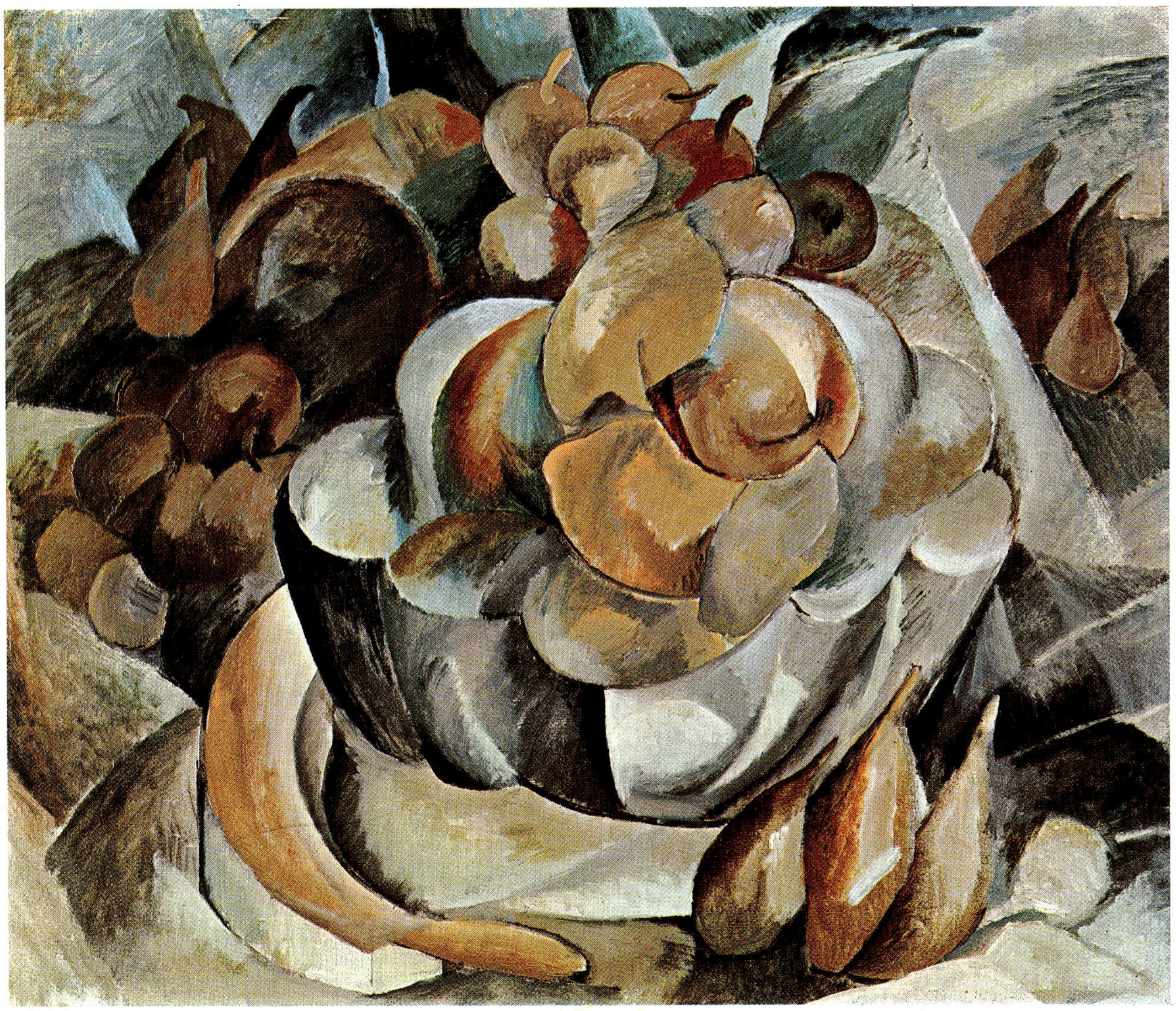

Georges Braque: *Still Life with Fruit Bowl*, 1908-1909

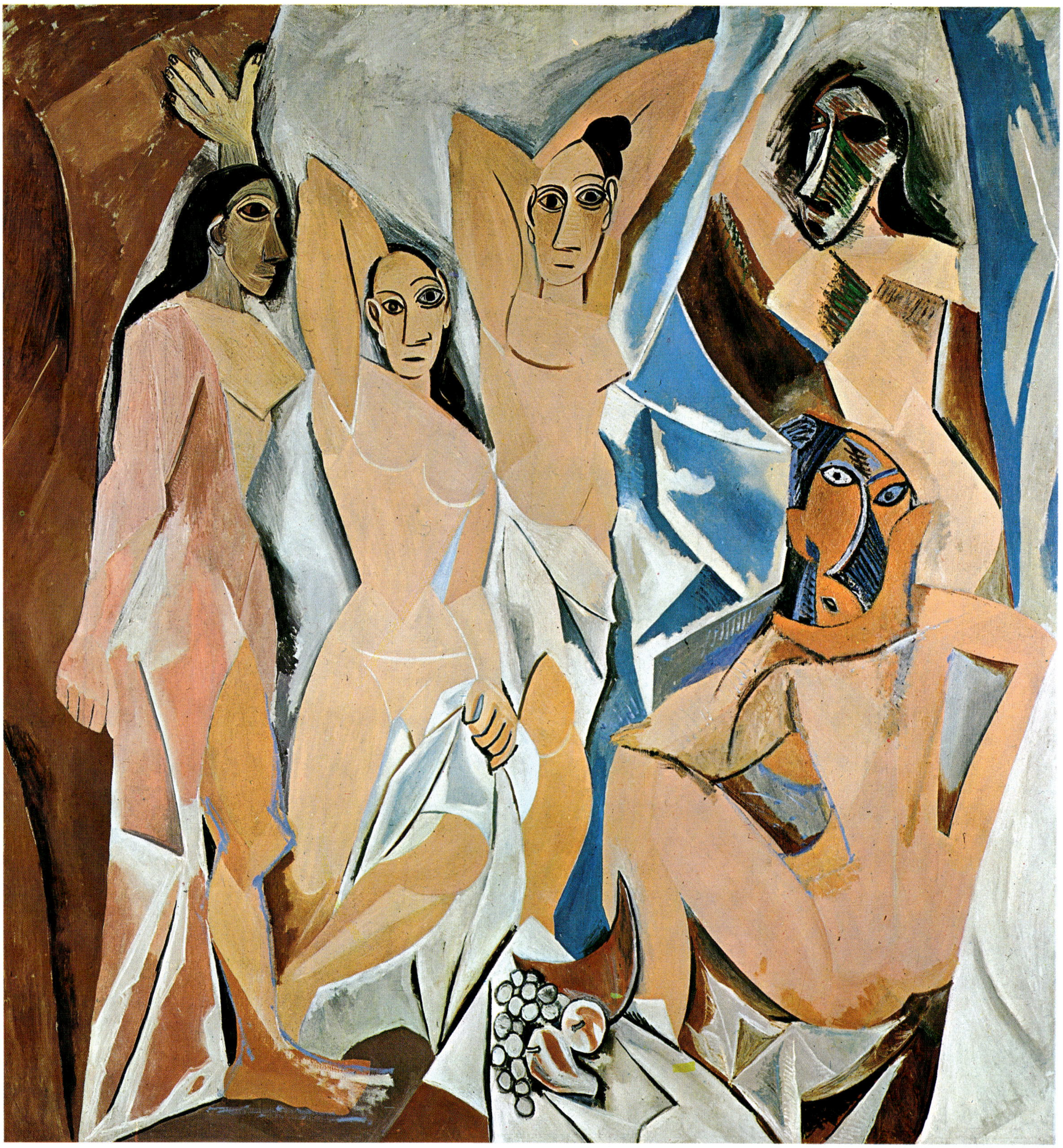

Pablo Picasso: *Les Demoiselles d'Aviignon,* 1907

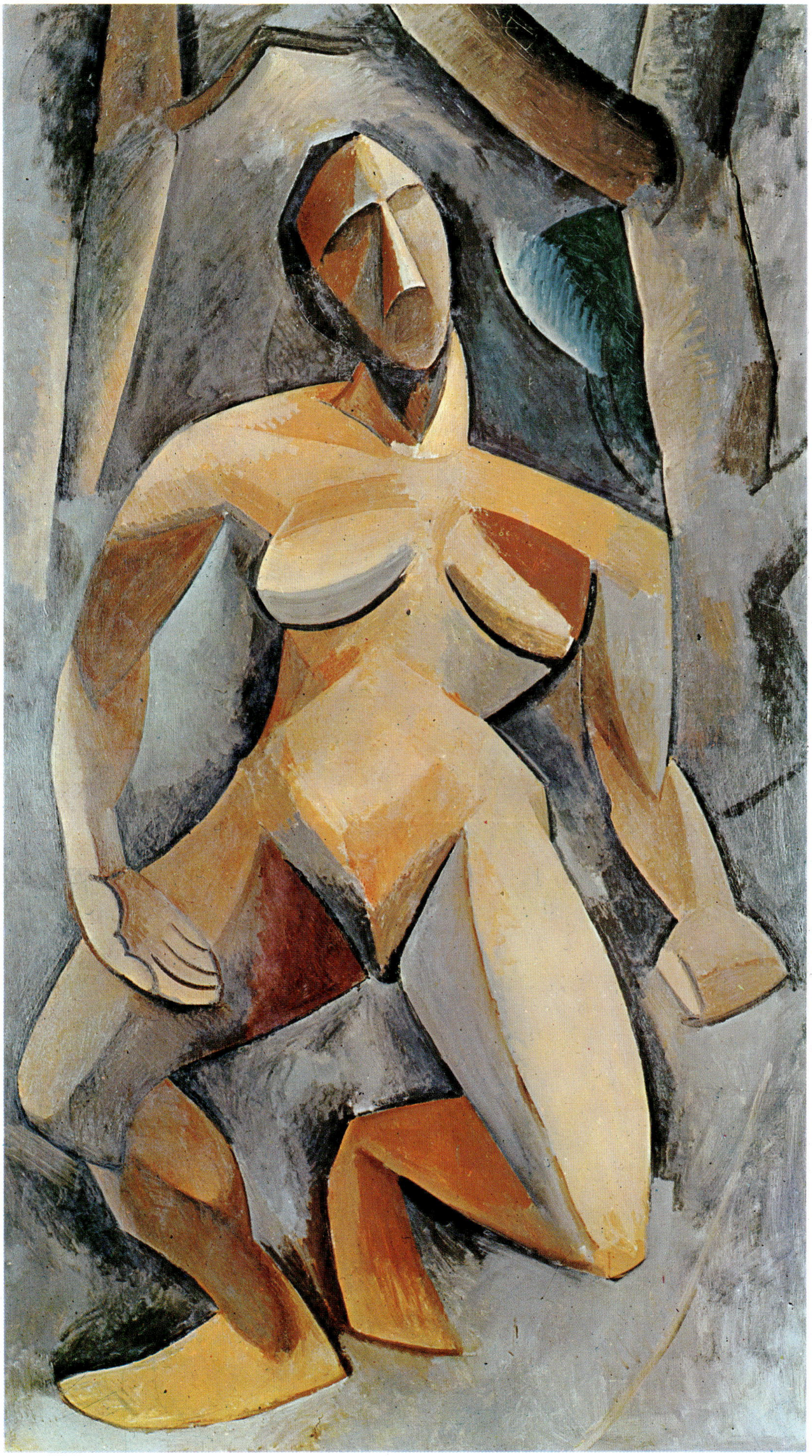

Pablo Picasso: *Dryad,* 1908

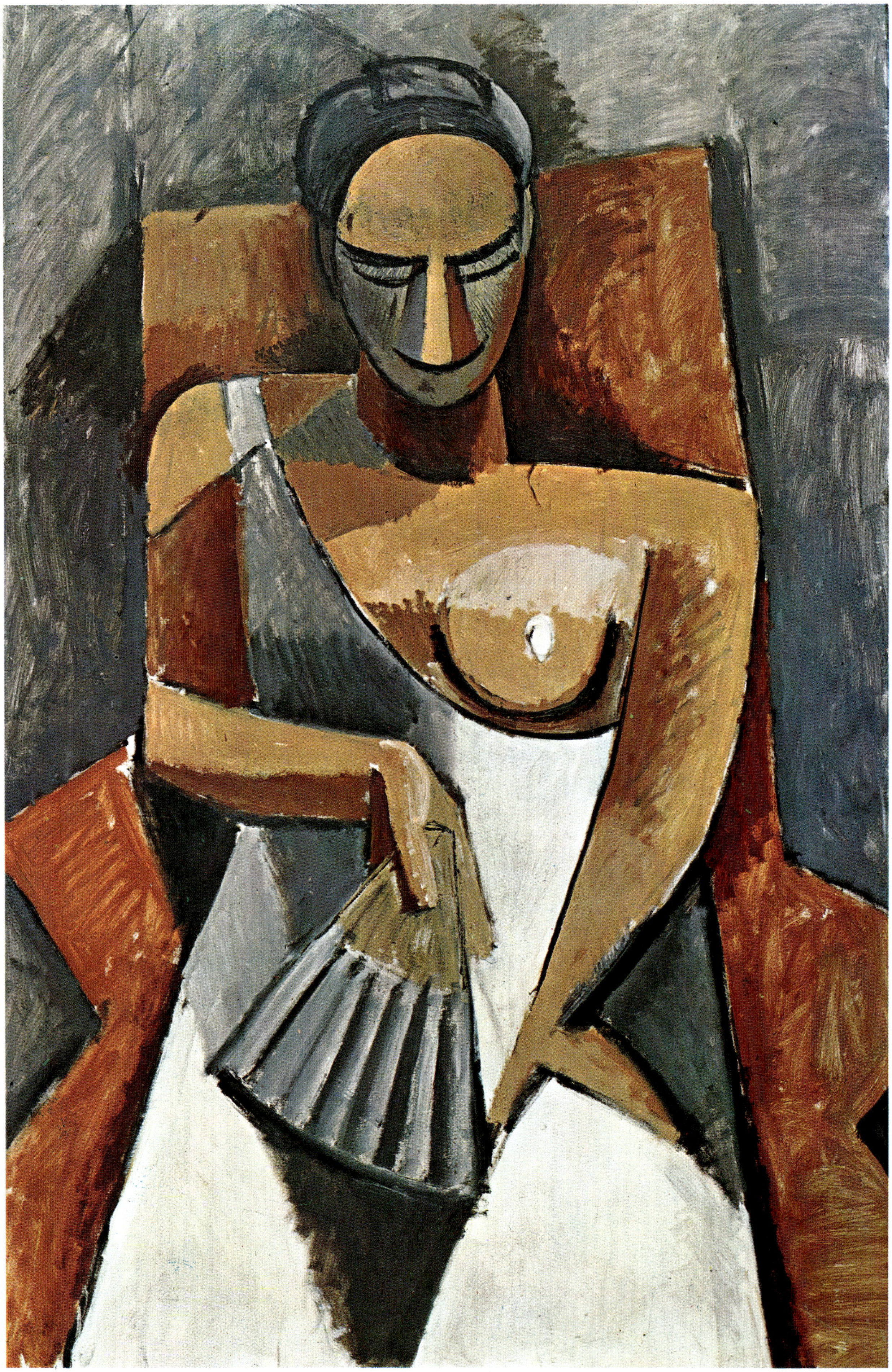

Pablo Picasso: *Woman with a Fan,* 1908

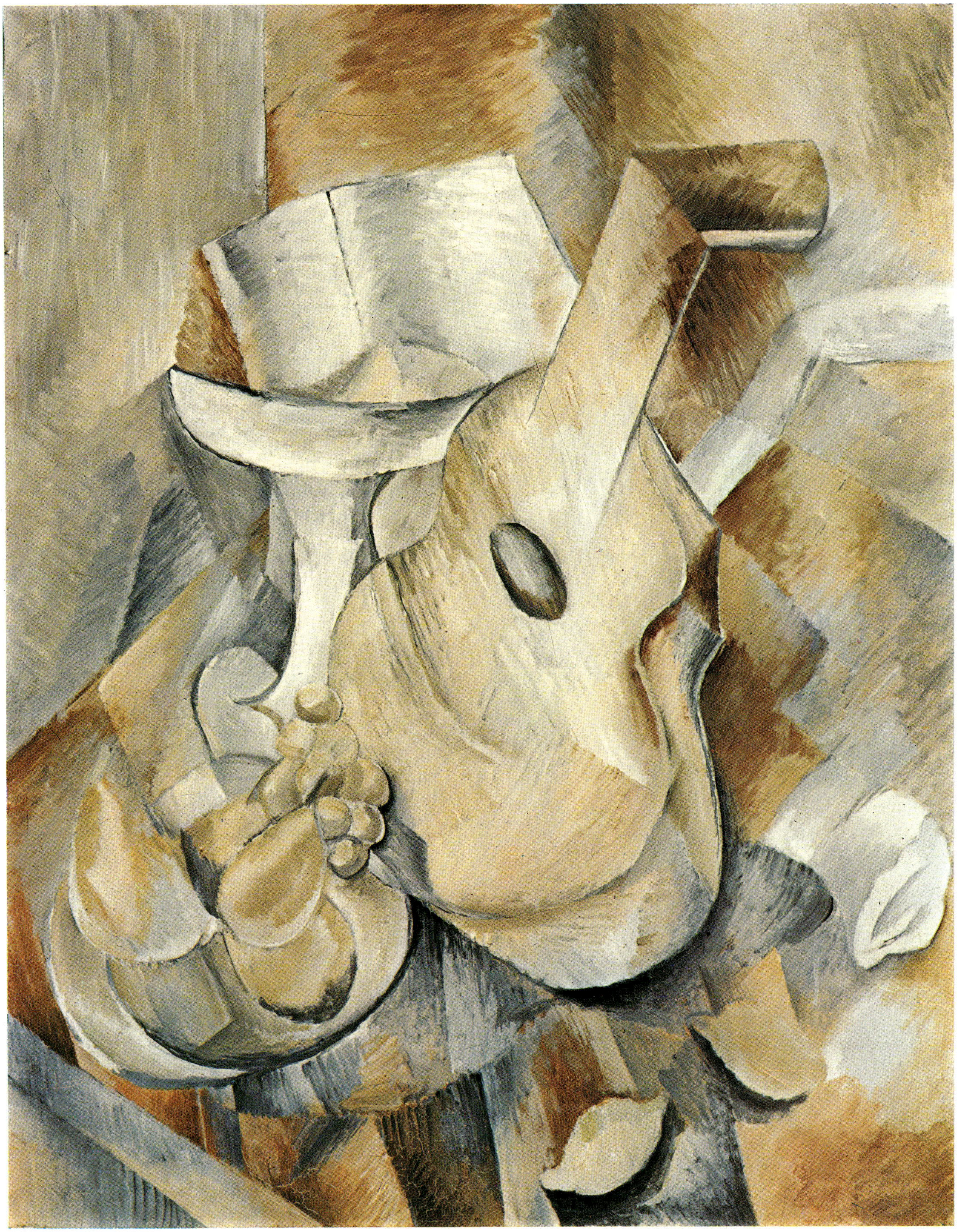

Georges Braque: *Guitar and Compote*, 1909

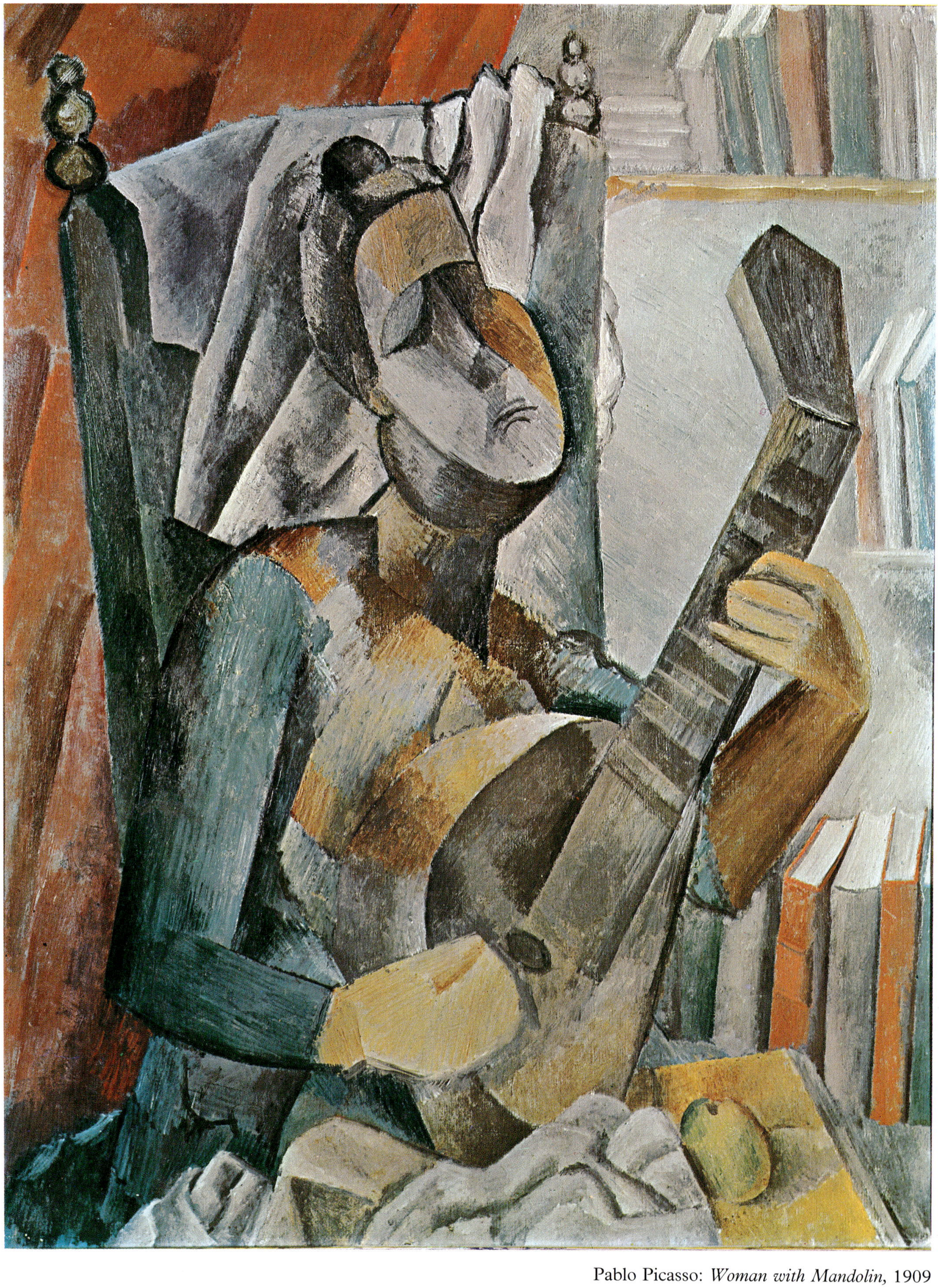

Pablo Picasso: *Woman with Mandolin,* 1909

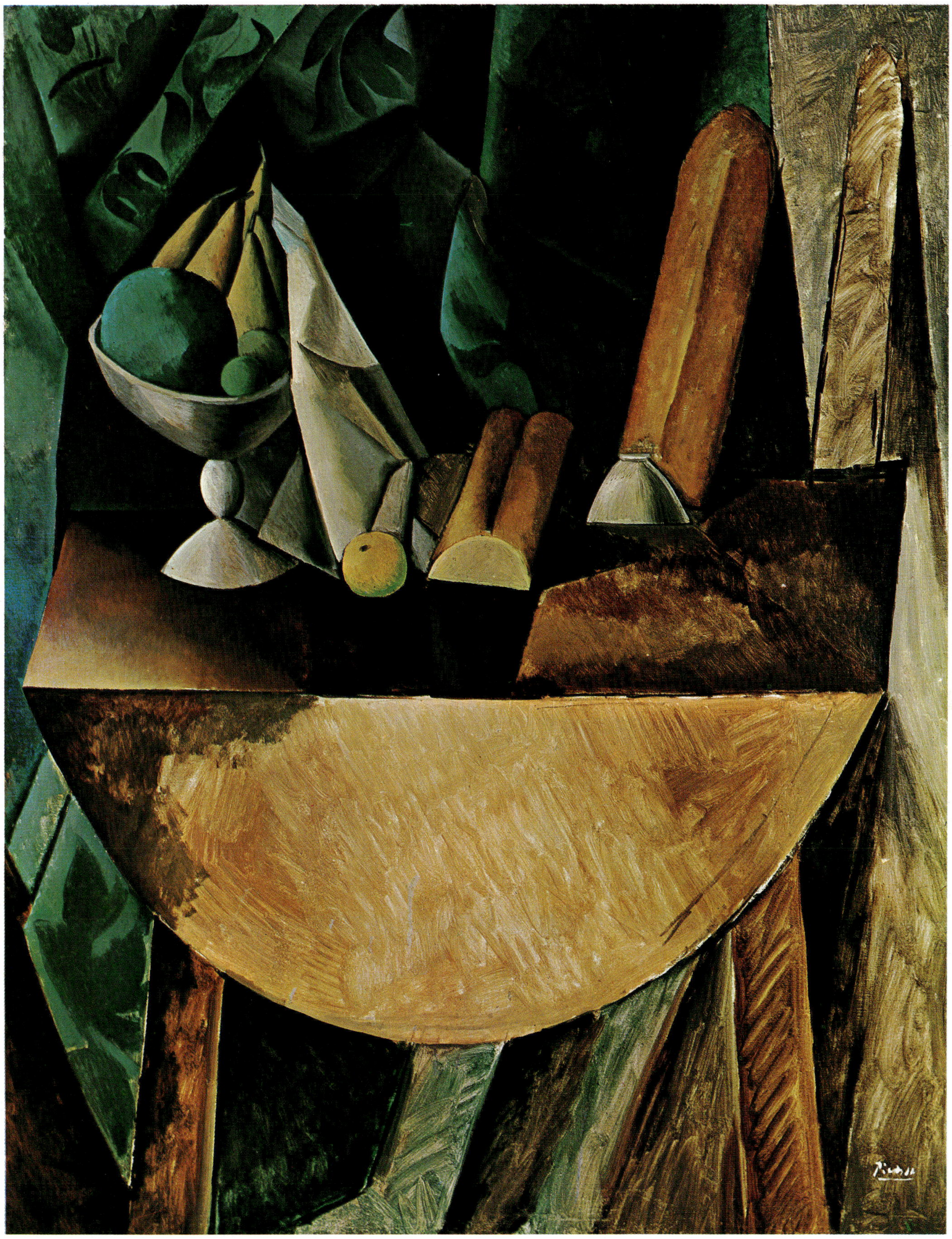

Pablo Picasso: *Bread and Fruit Dish on a Table,* 1908

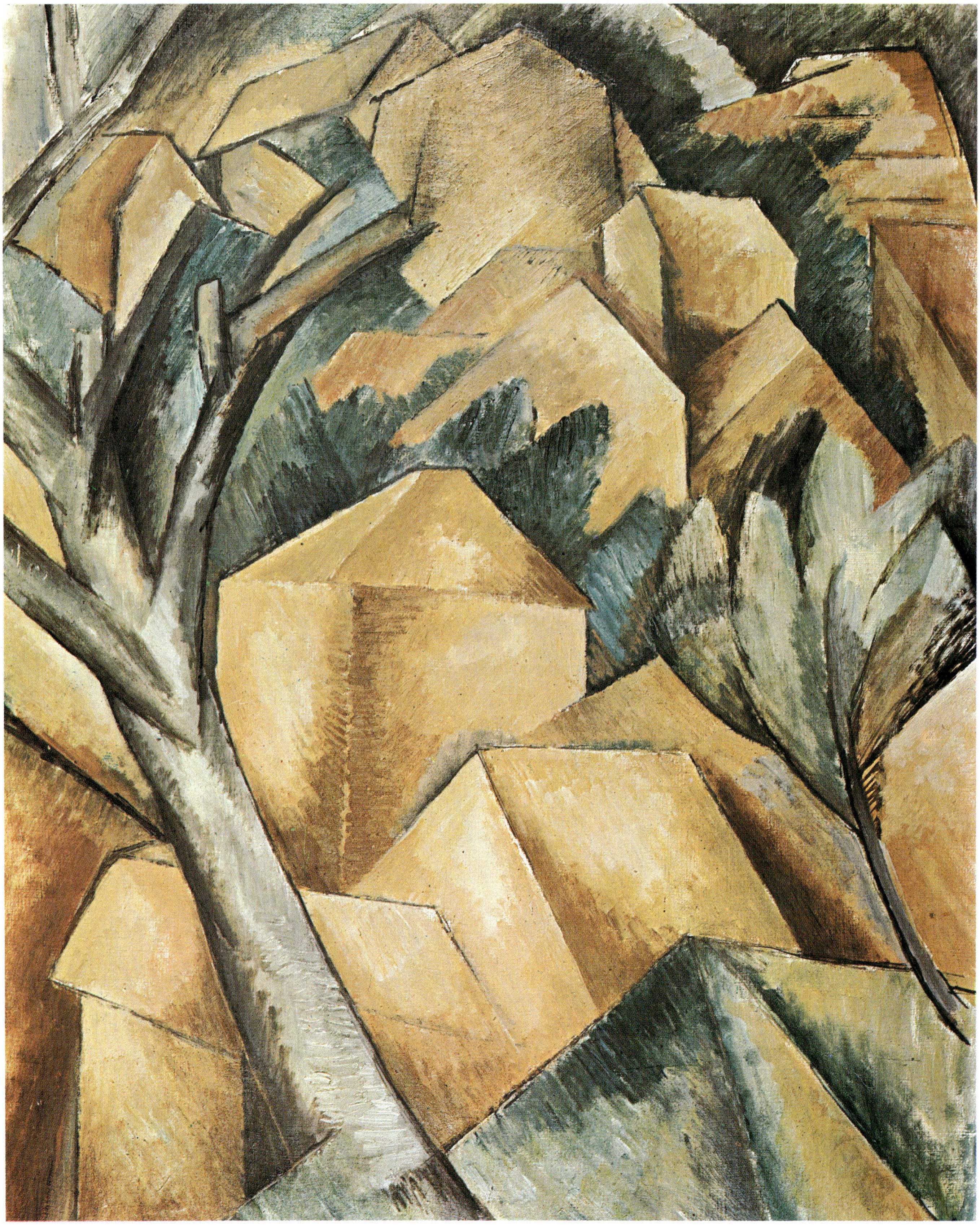

Georges Braque: *Houses at L'Estaque*, 1908

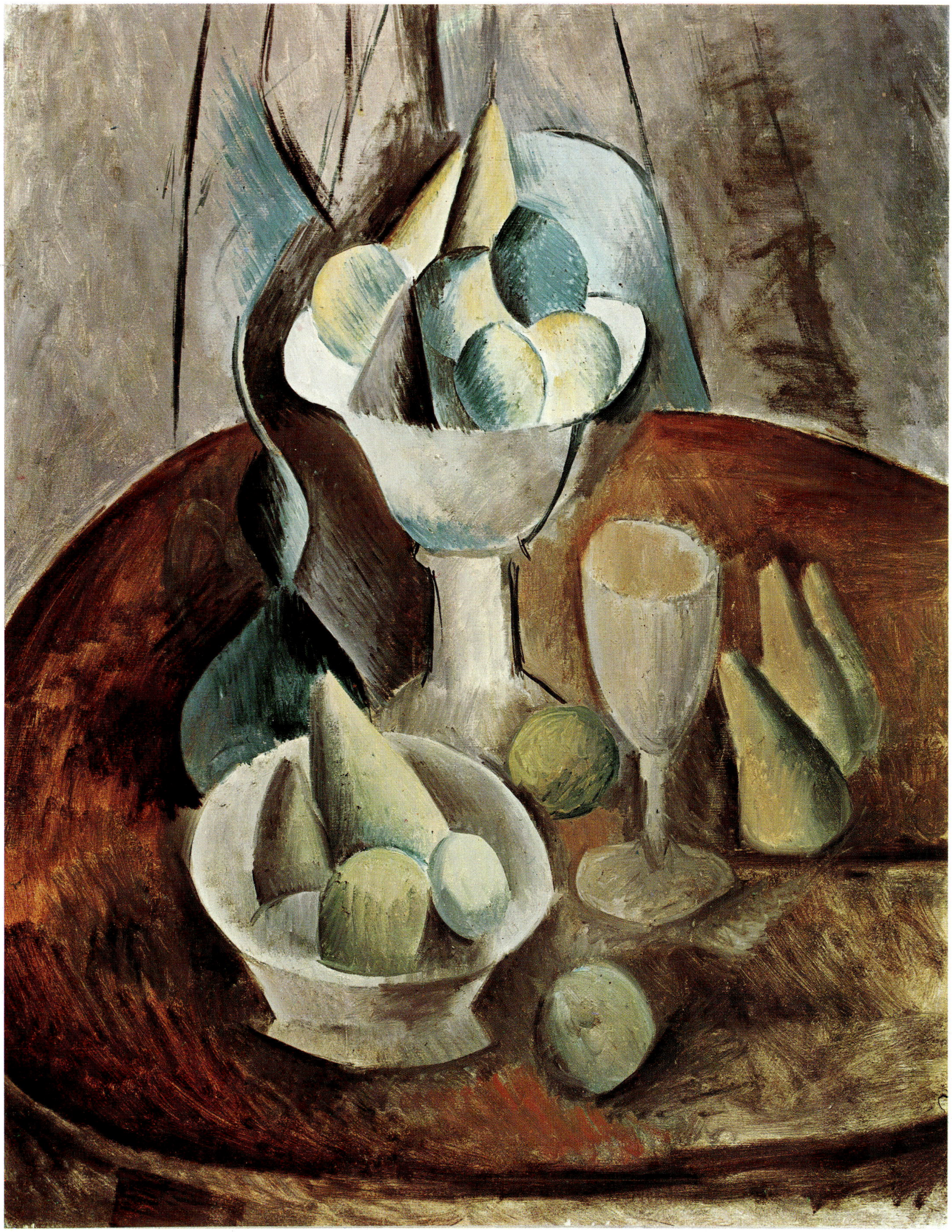

Pablo Picasso: *Compote with Pears,* 1909

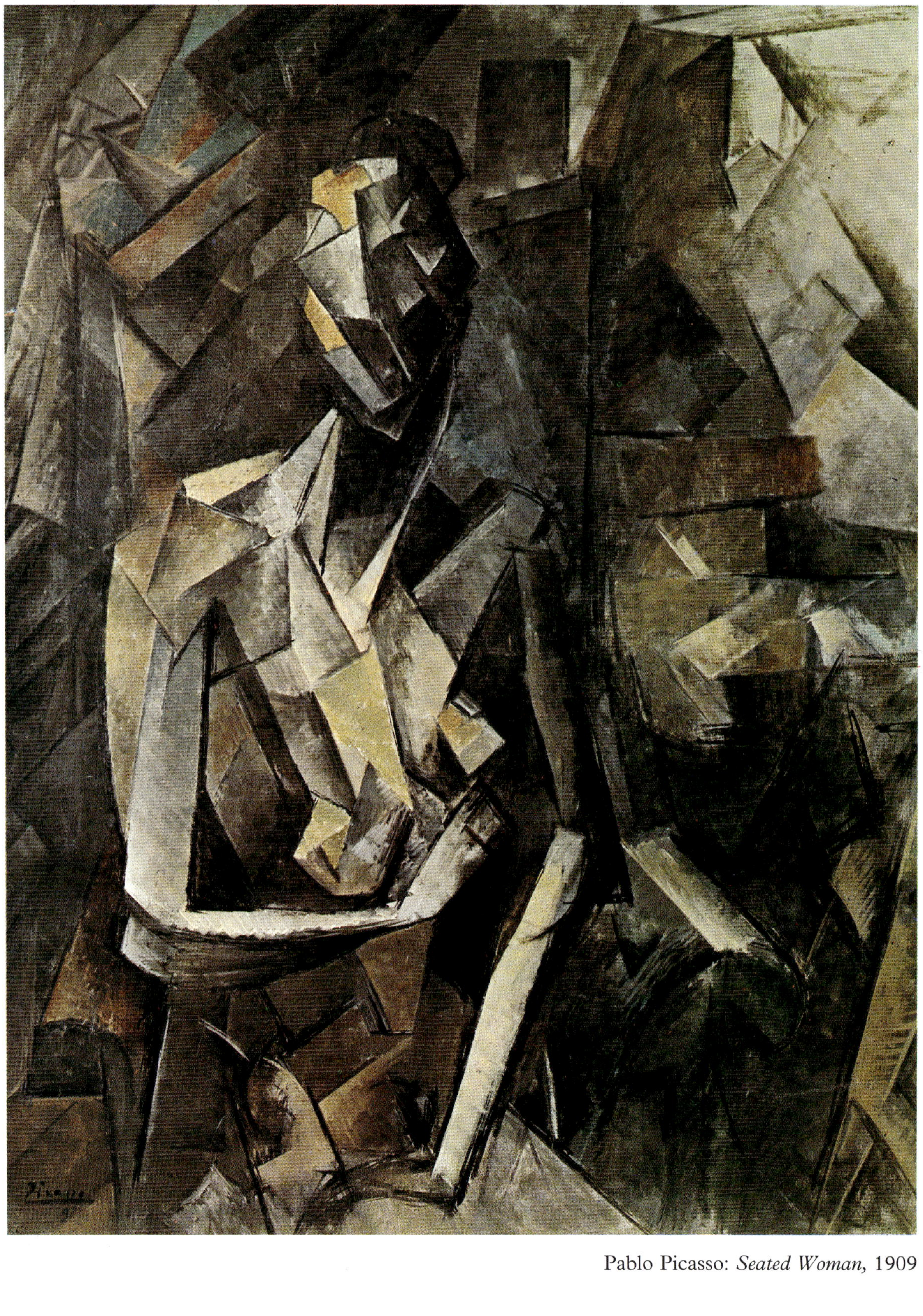

Pablo Picasso: *Seated Woman,* 1909

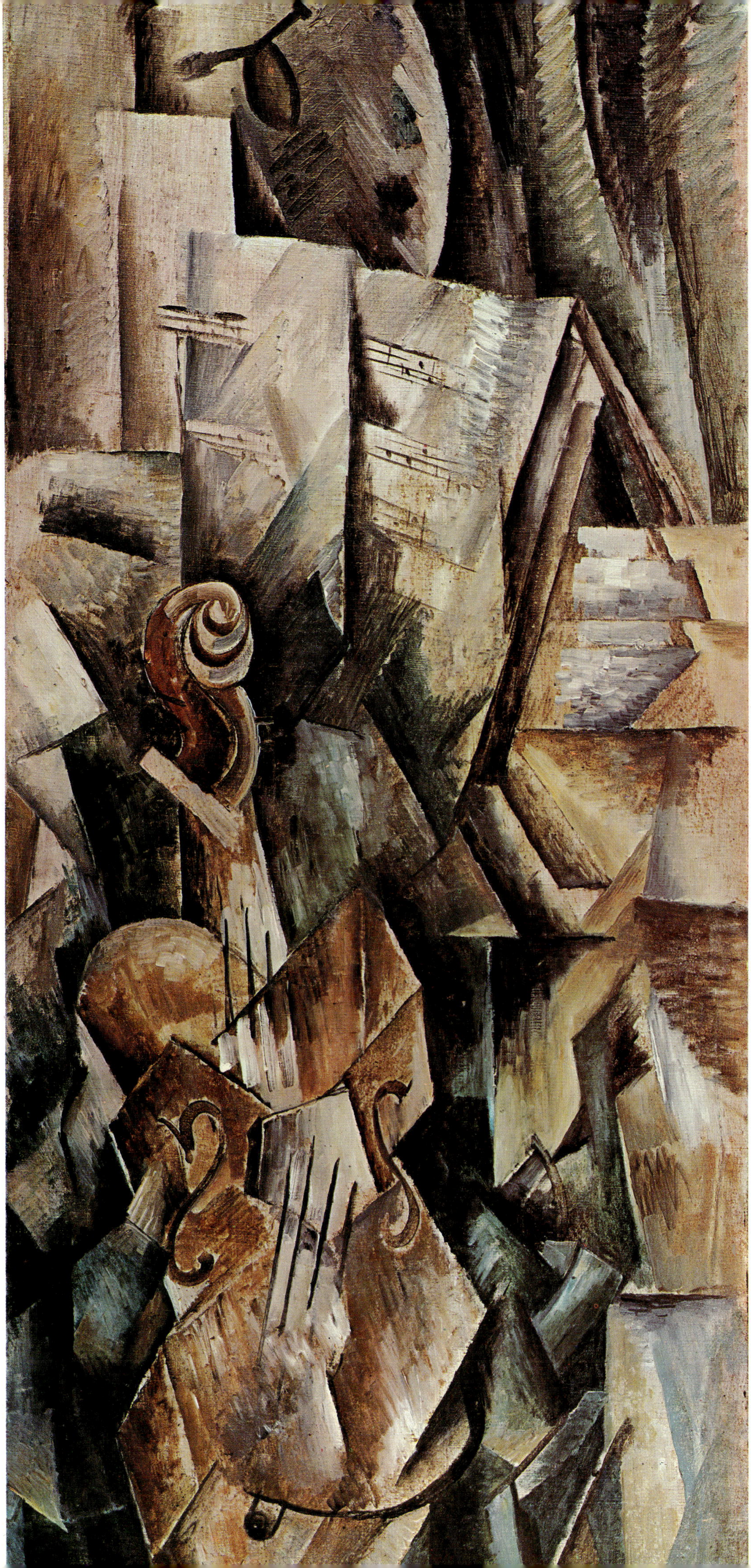

Georges Braque:
Violin and Palette, 1910

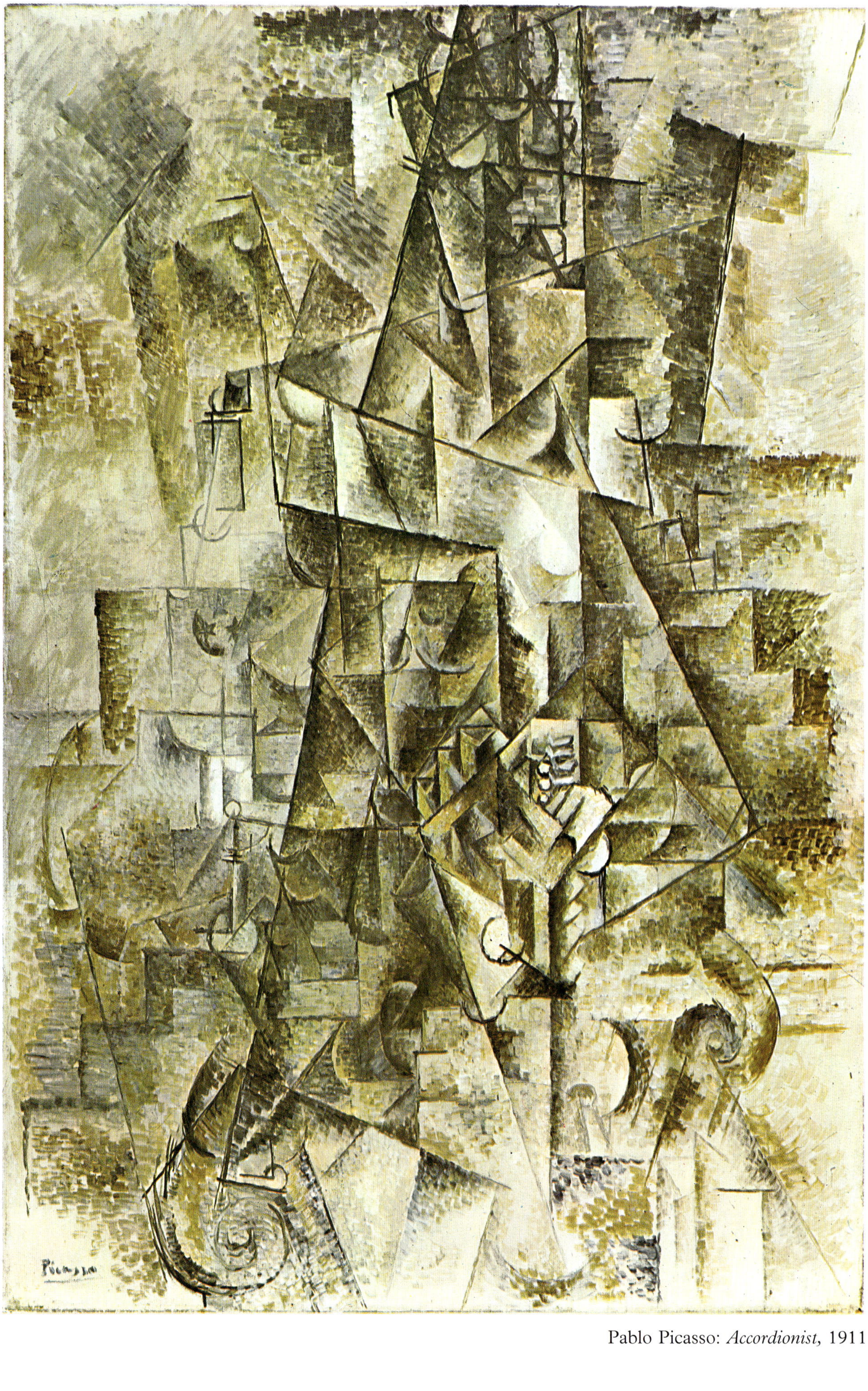

Pablo Picasso: *Accordionist,* 1911

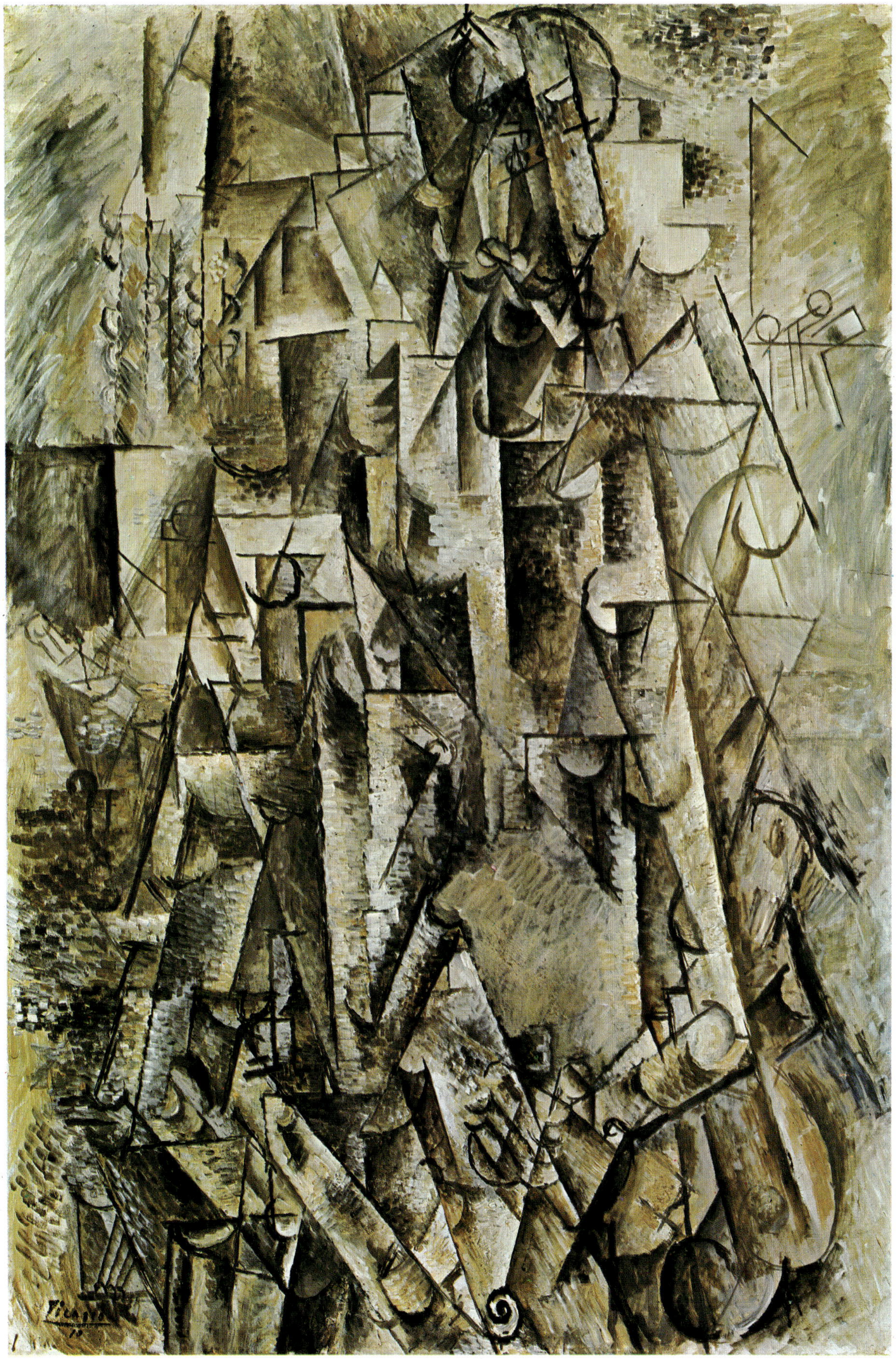

Pablo Picasso: *The Poet,* 1911

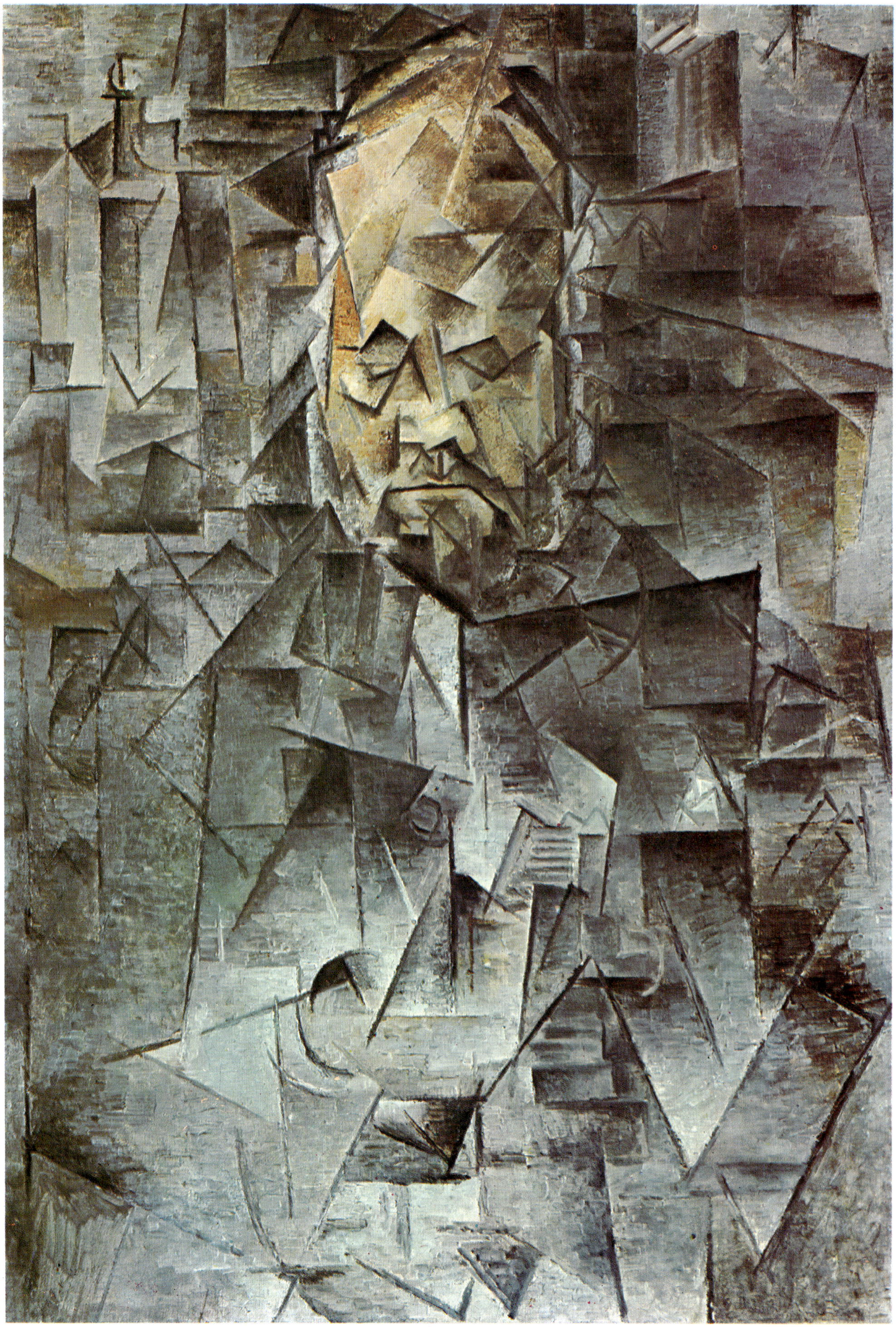

Pablo Picasso: *Portrait of Ambroise Vollard* , 1909-1910

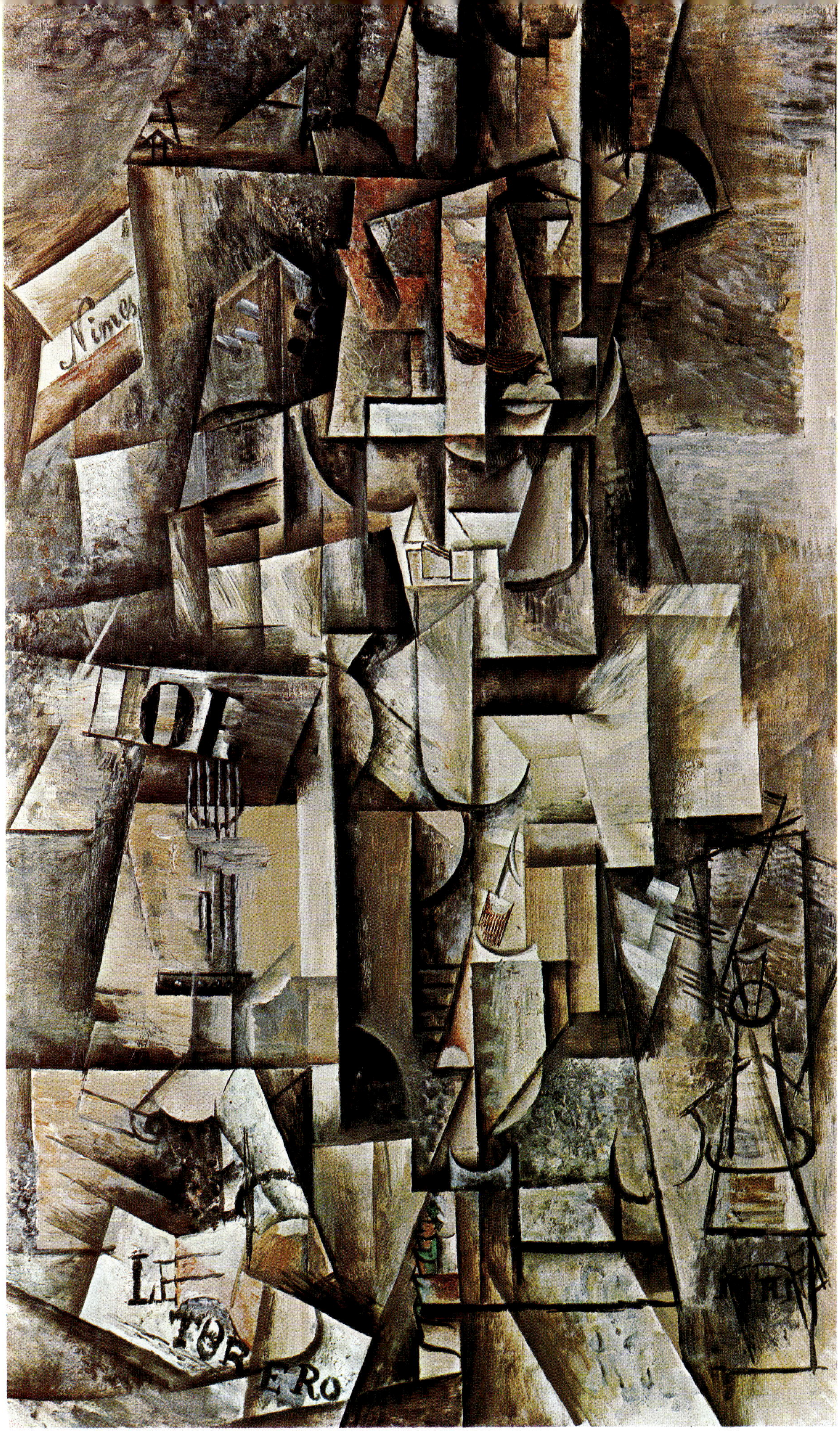

Pablo Picasso: *The Aficionado (Le Torero)*, 1912

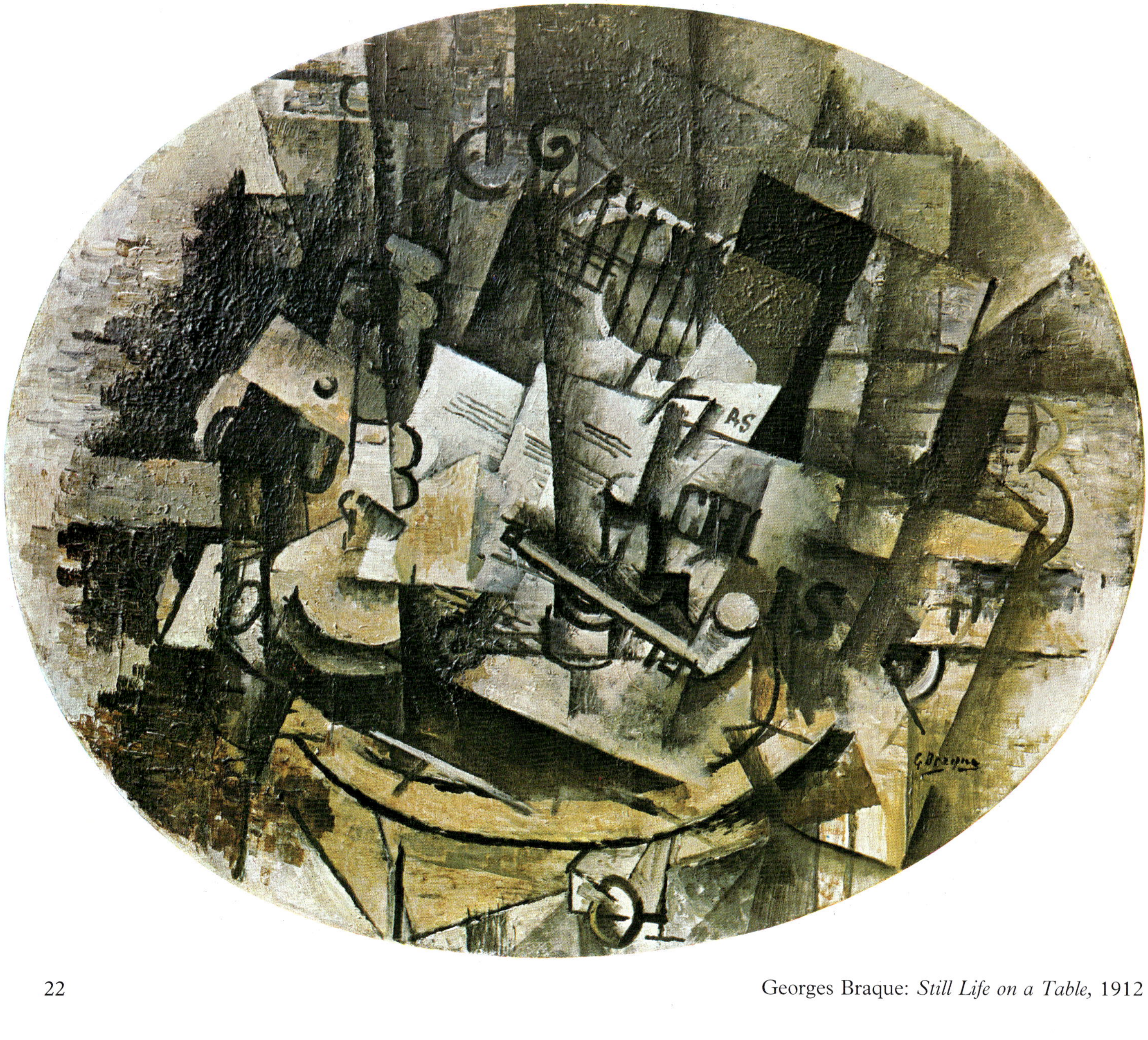

Georges Braque: *Still Life on a Table*, 1912

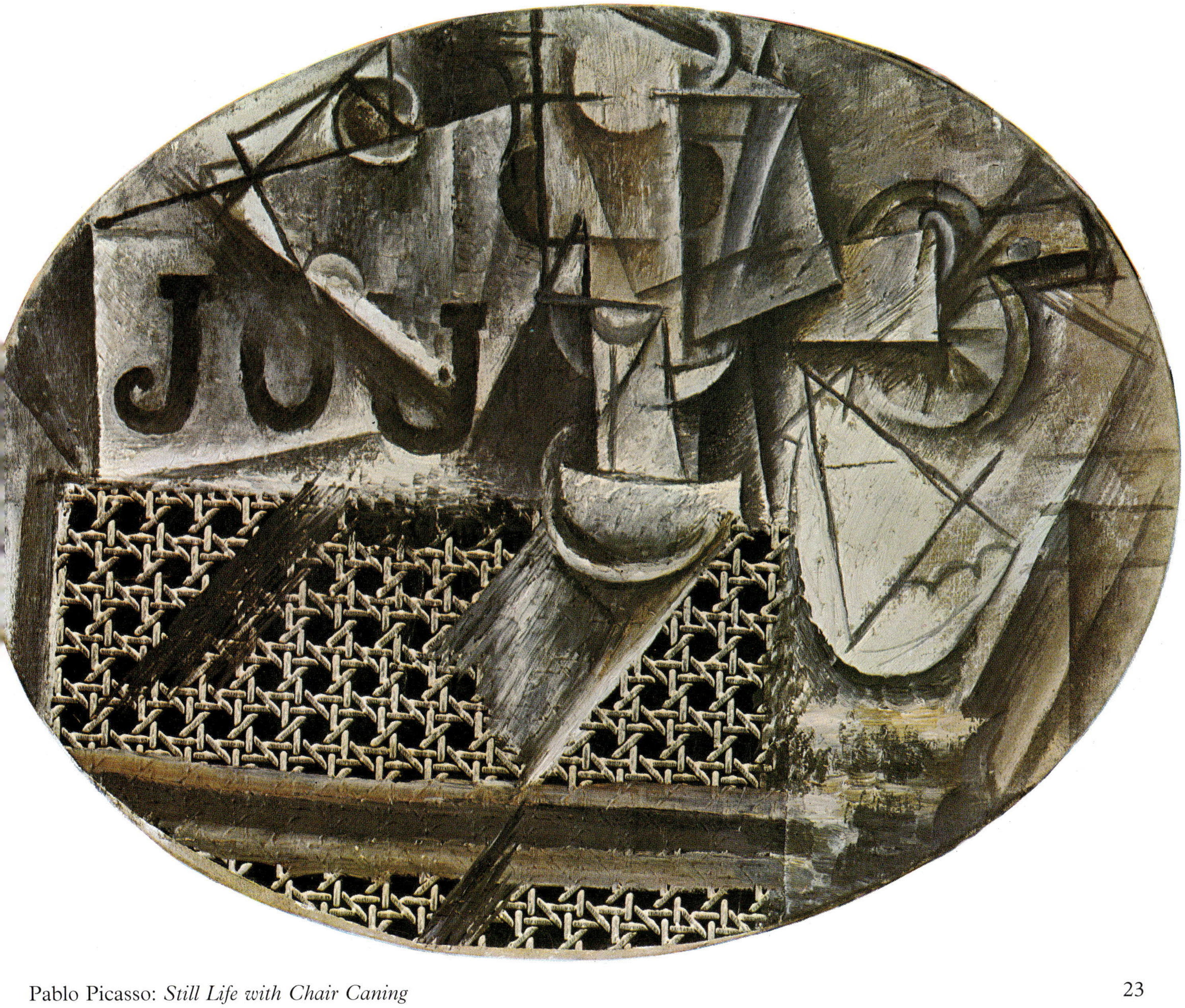

Pablo Picasso: *Still Life with Chair Caning*

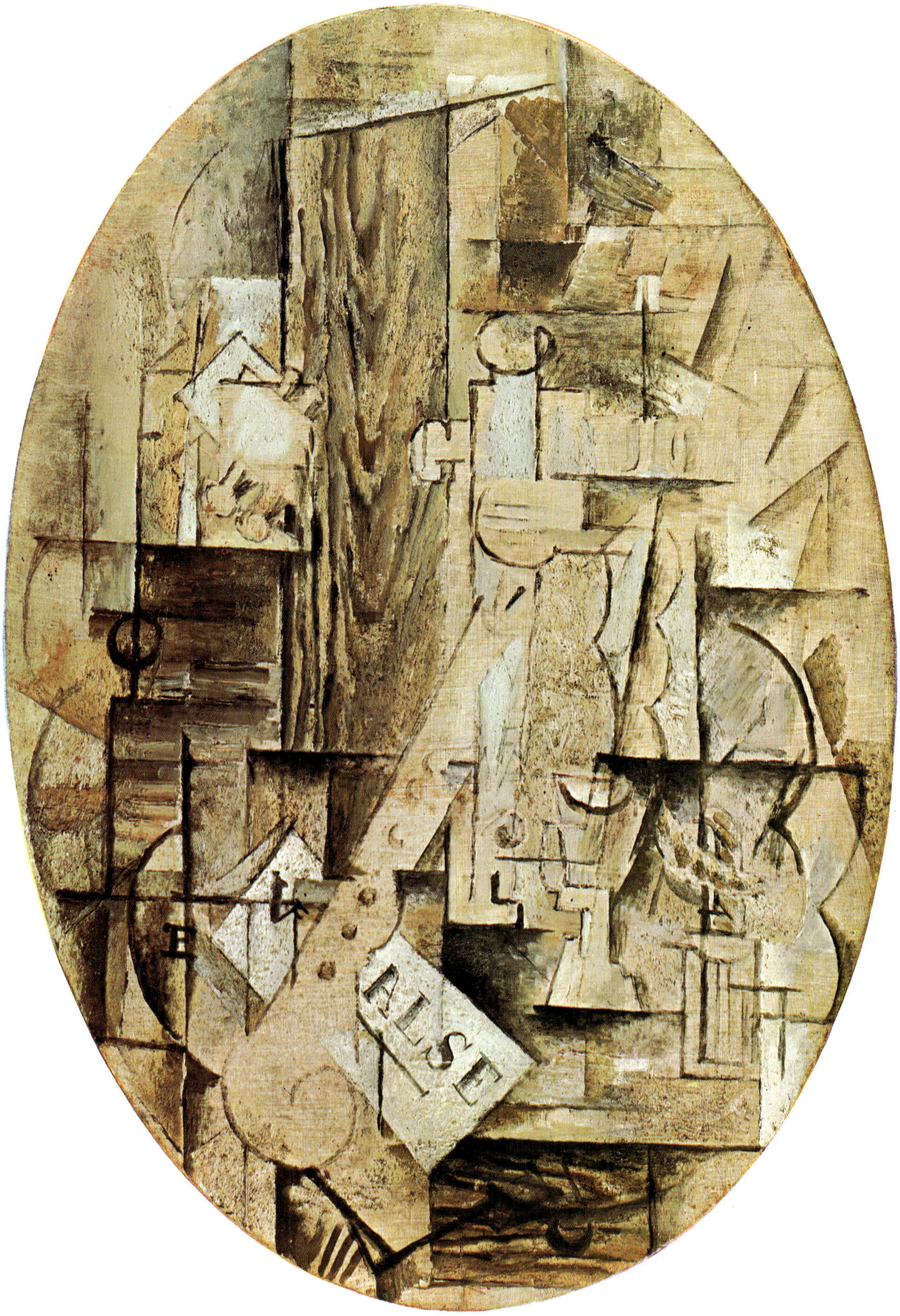

George Braque: *Still Life (Valse)*, 1912

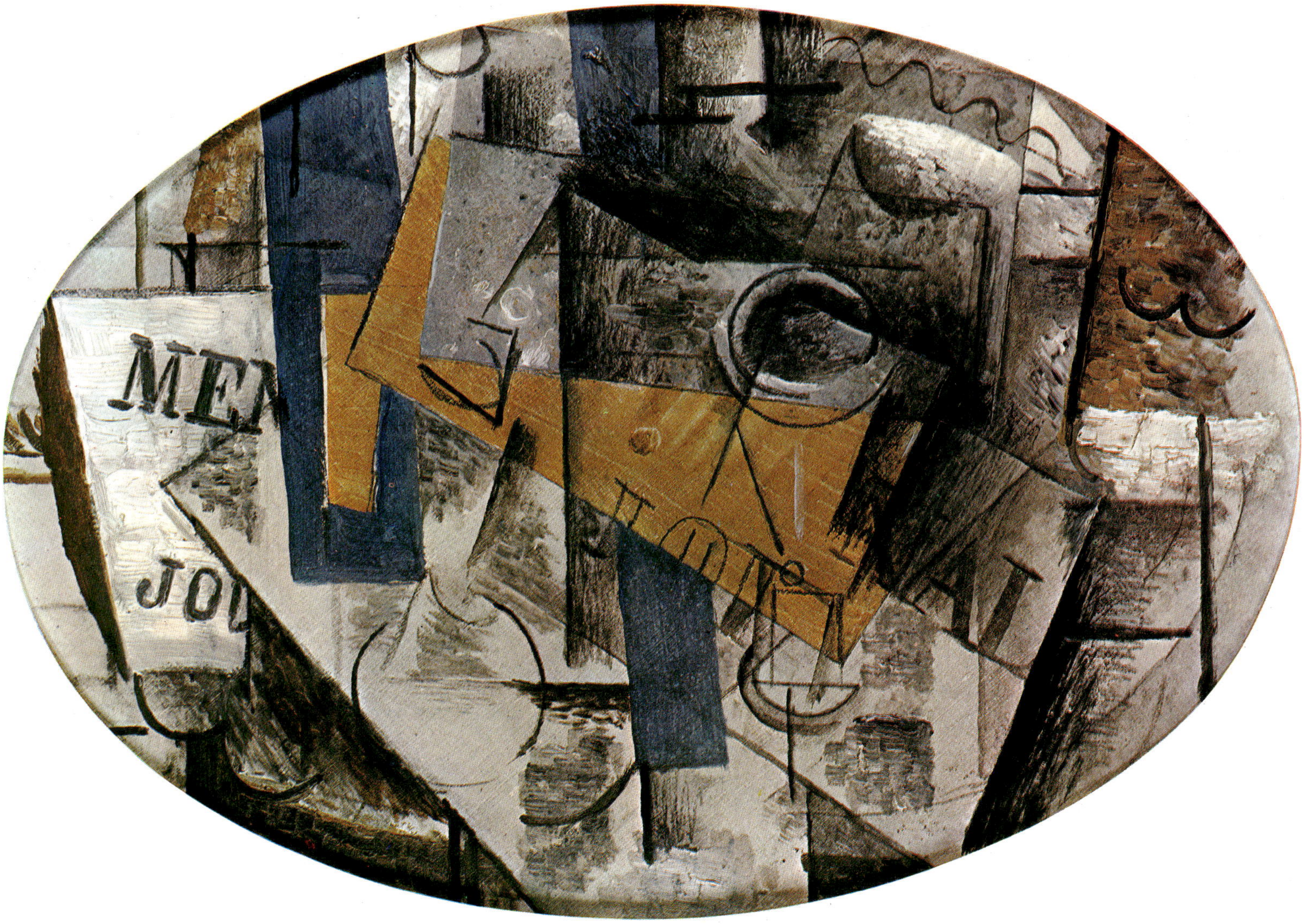

George Braque: *Glass and Newspaper,* 1913

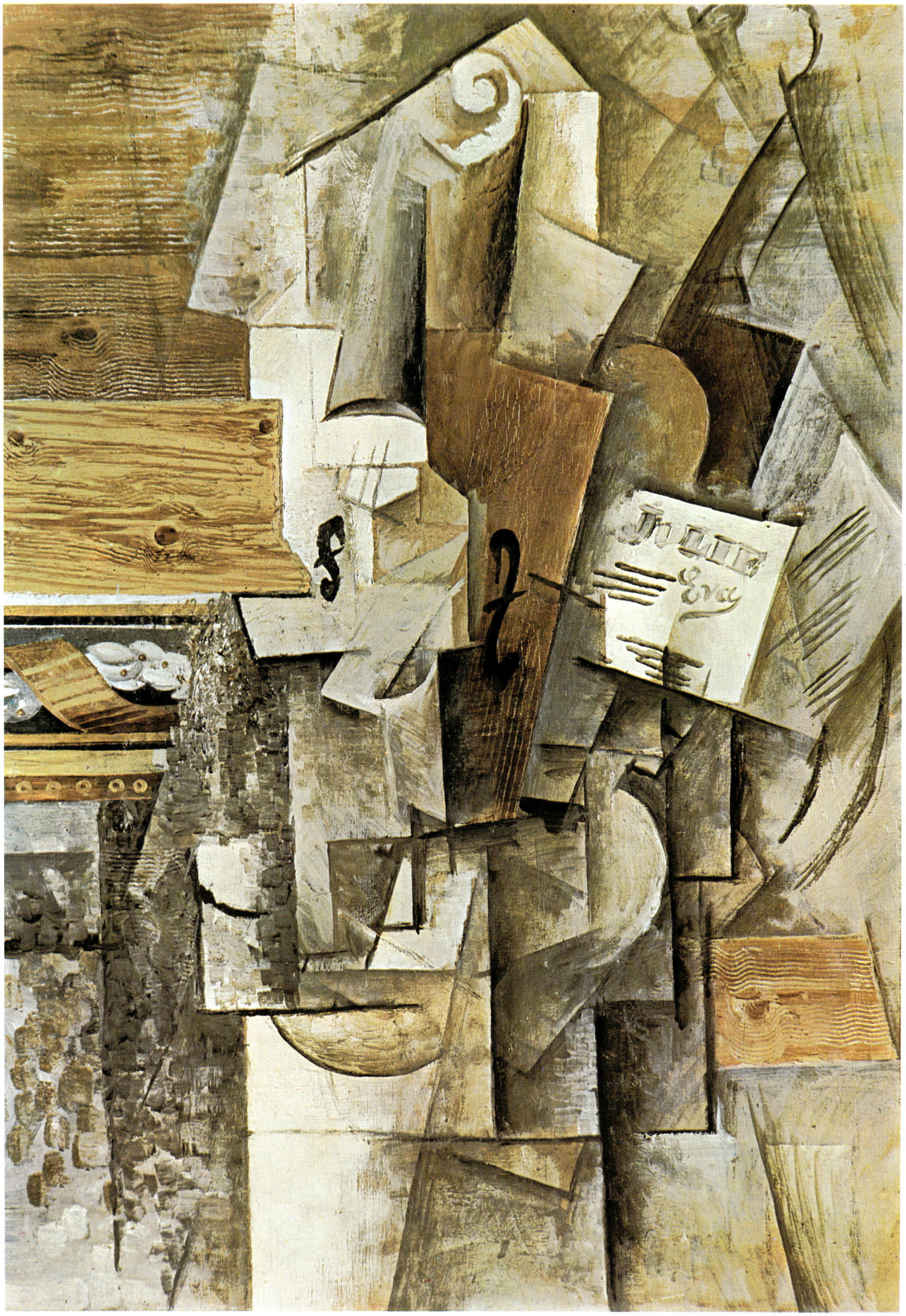

Pablo Picasso: *The Violin (Jolie Eva)* 1912

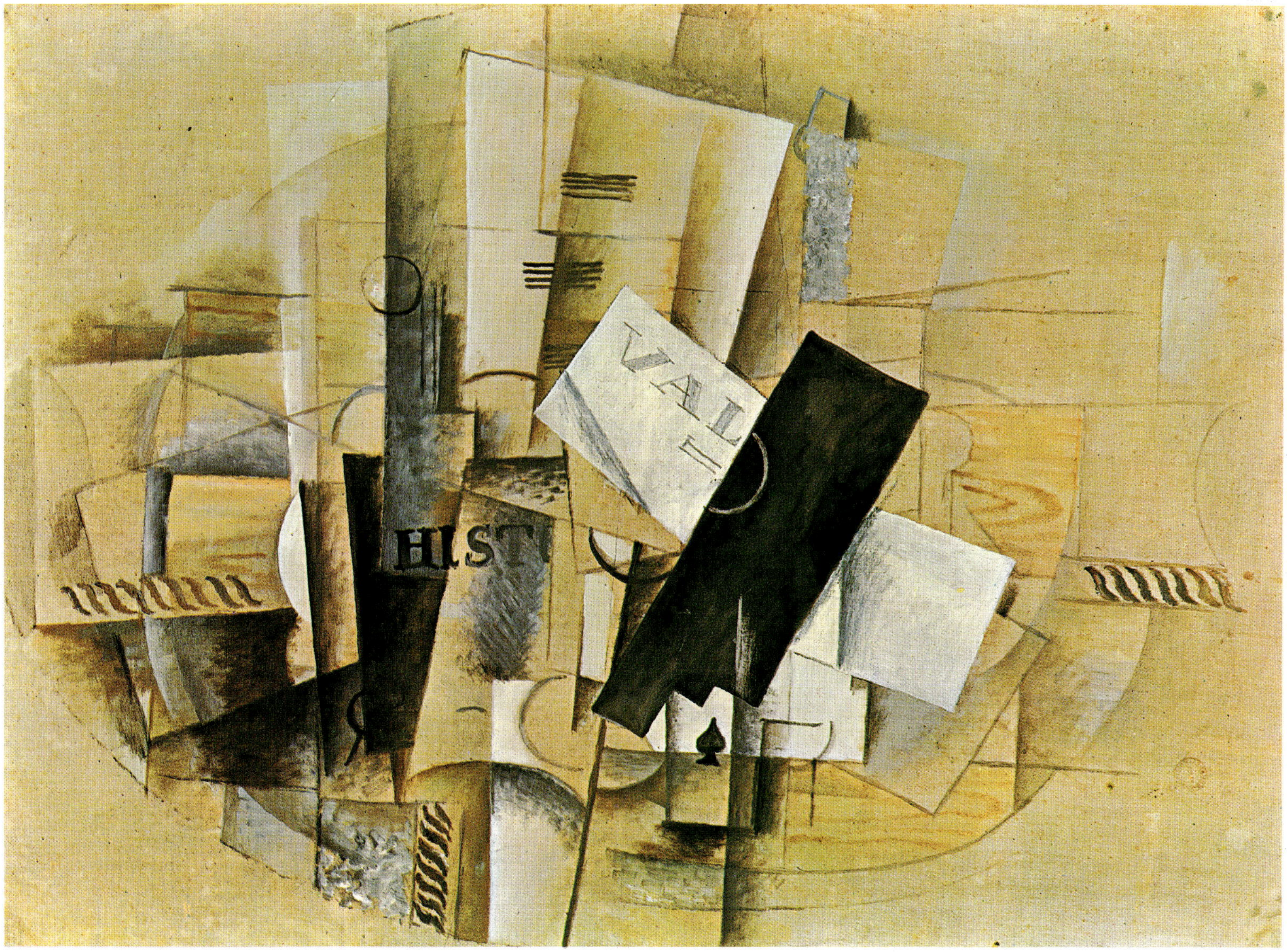

George Braque: *The Musician's Table,* 1913

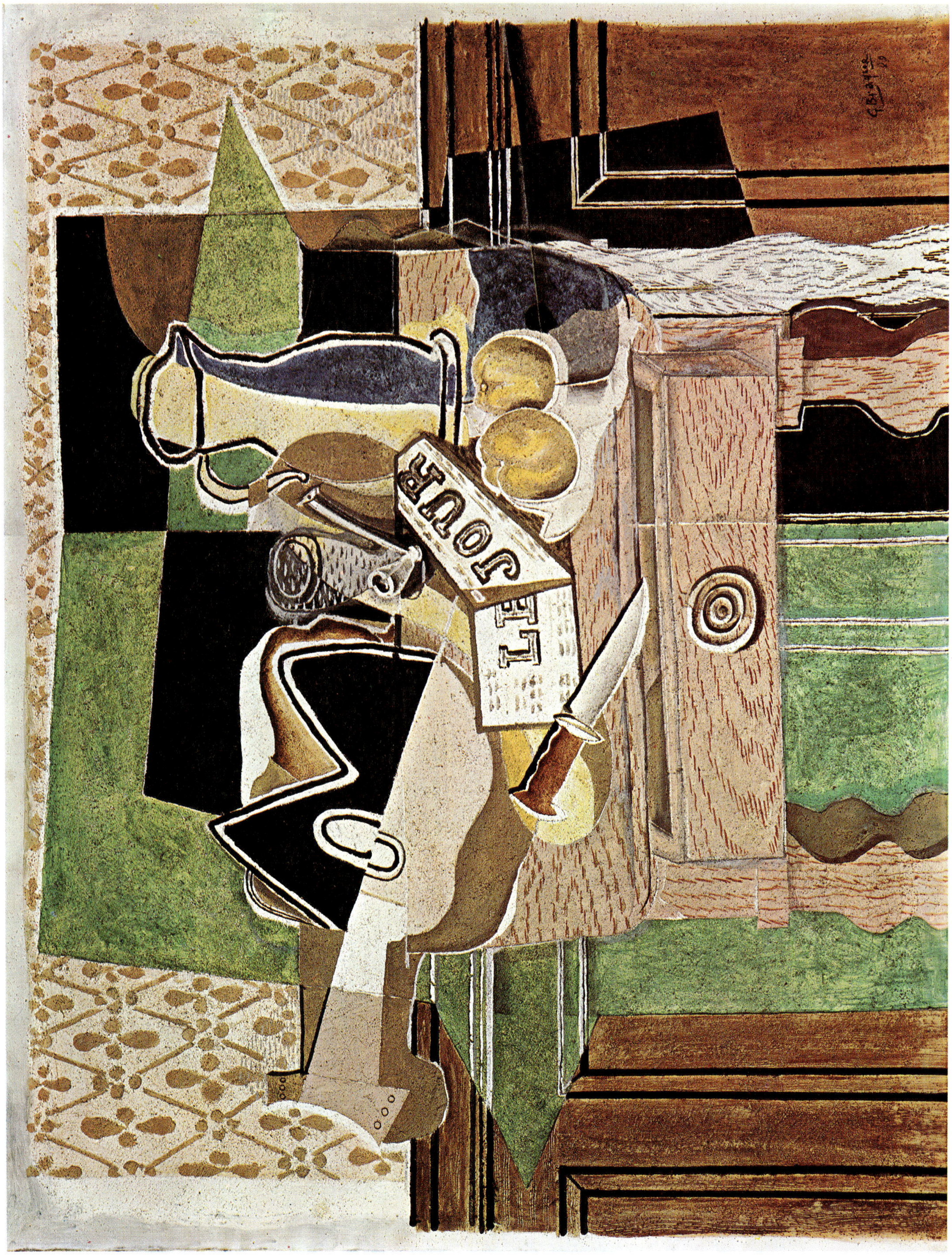

George Braque: *Still Life: Le Jour*, 1929

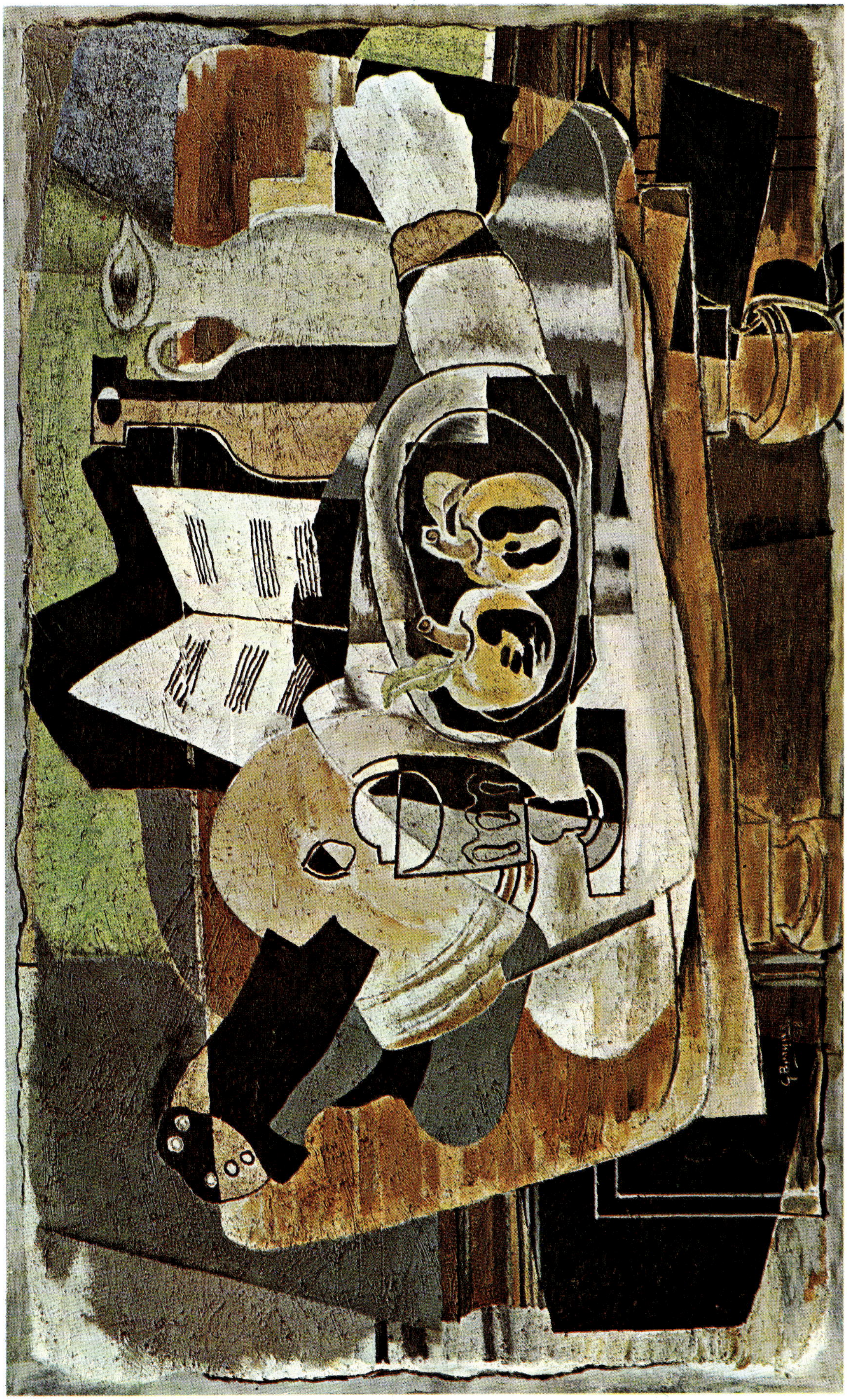

George Braque: *Still Life: The Table*, 1928

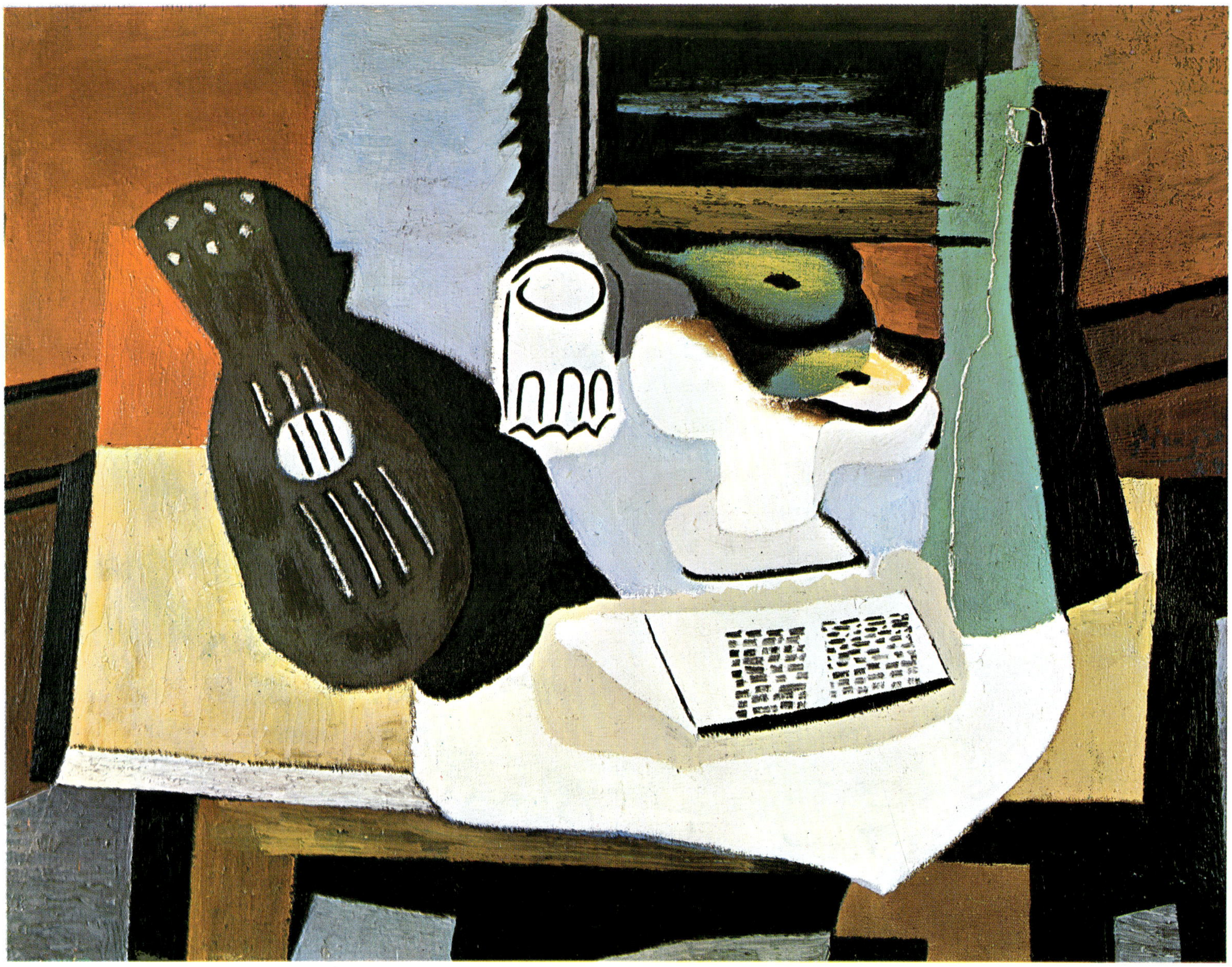

Pablo Picasso: *Guitar, Glass and Fruit Bowl,* 1924

Juan Gris Apart from Picasso and Braque, the prime movers, there were other artists working within Cubism, the most significant Juan Gris (1887-1927). Gris acknowledged his debt to Cézanne but declared, "Cézanne goes toward architecture. I start out from it." He stated that his aim was "to create new combinations of known elements." Occupying a studio in the "floating laundry" in 1907, Gris witnessed the very beginnings of Cubism, though he expressed the ideas of the movement in a way completely different from Picasso and Braque.

What we find in his *Portrait of Picasso*, first exhibited at the Salon des Artistes Indépendants in 1912, is absolutely no attempt at representation but the interplay of light with planes and edges. Picasso's words also apply to Gris: "When I paint a picture I am not concerned with the fact that two people may be represented in it. Those people once existed for me but they exist no longer. My vision of them gave me an initial emotion, then little by little their presence became thinned.... then they disappeared altogether, or rather they became for me no longer people, but forms and colors." Gris's pictures contain cube-like forms, leading him to be described as "the most Cubist of the Cubists."

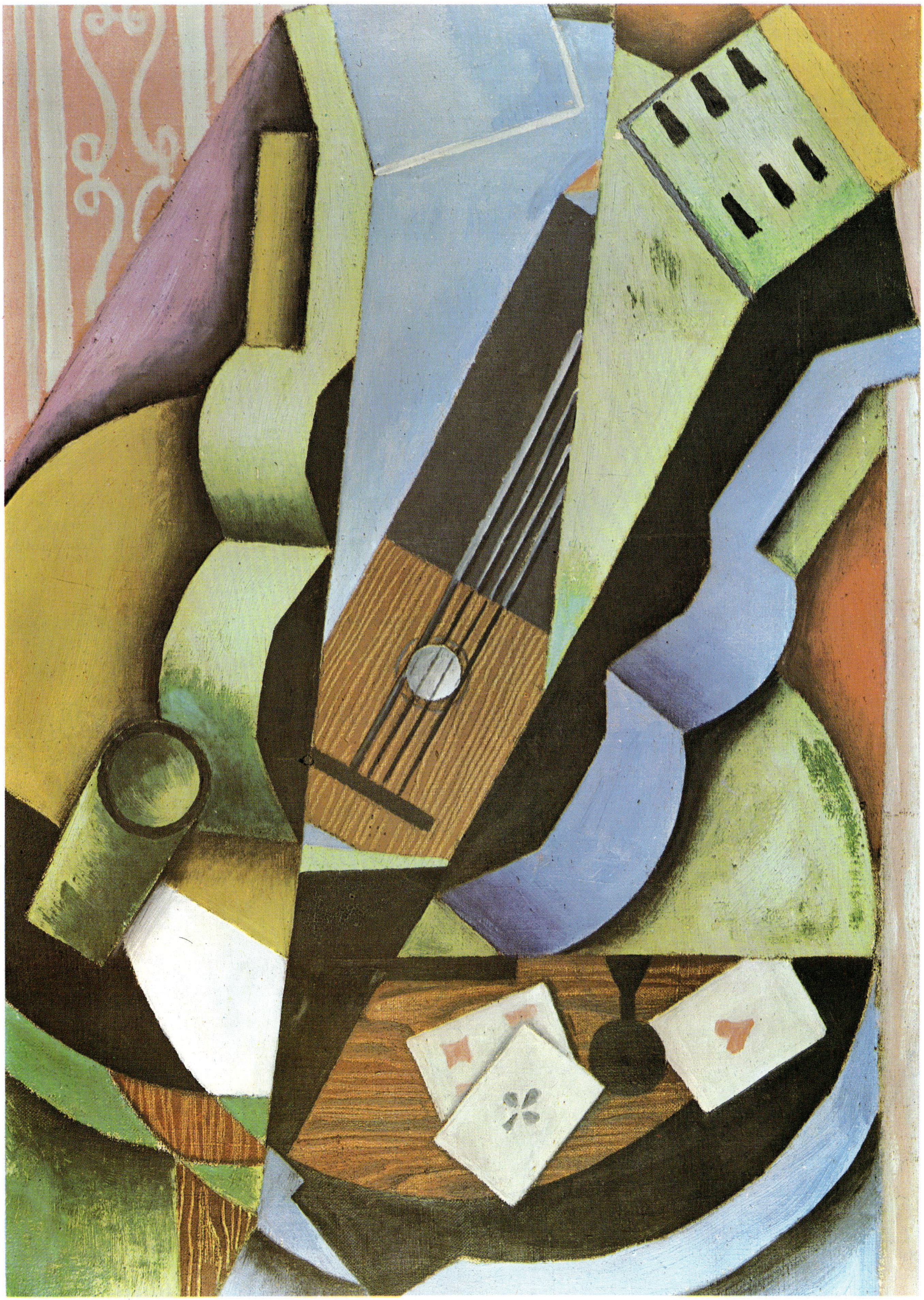

Juan Gris: *Three Cards,* 1913

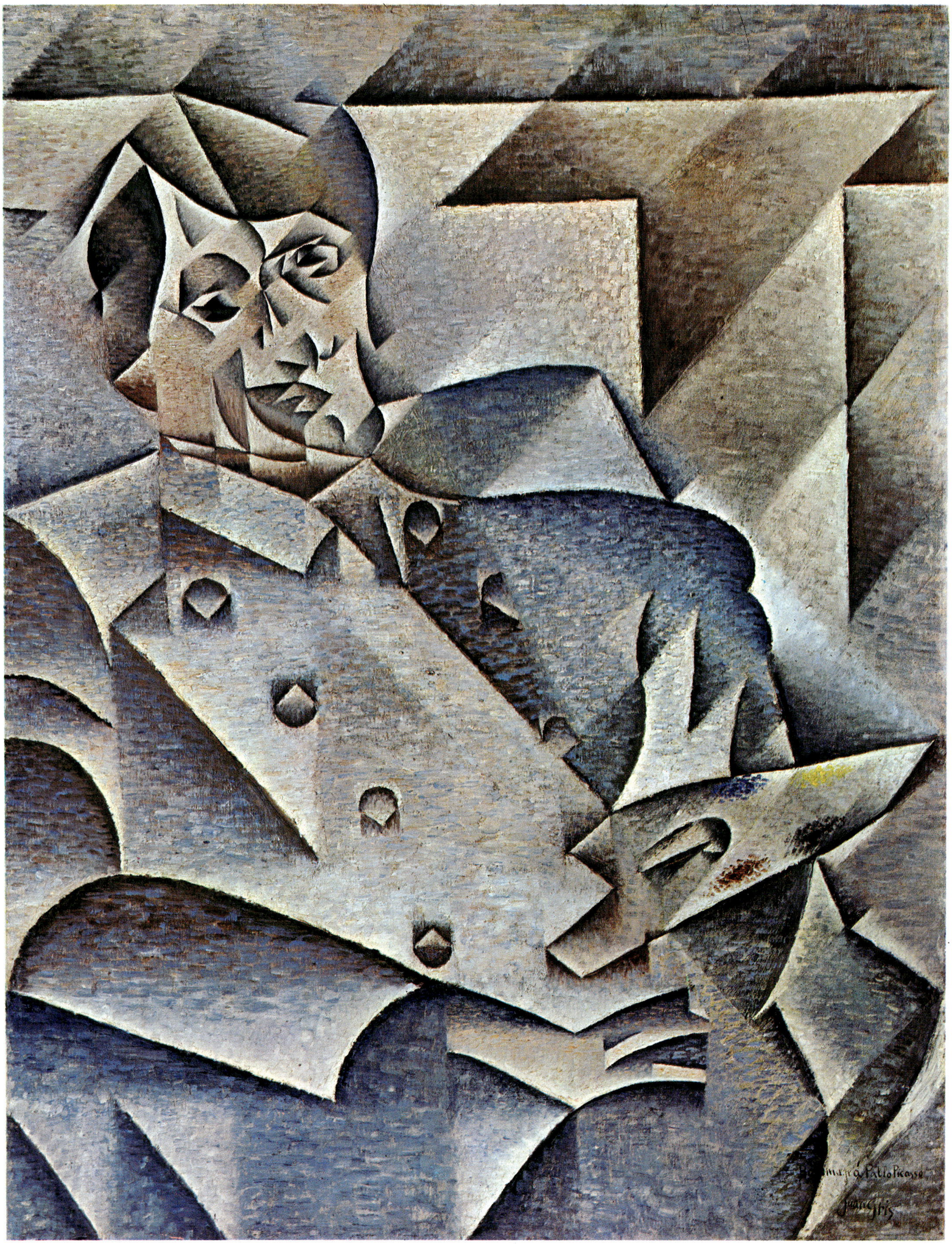

Juan Gris: *Portrait of Picasso,* 1912

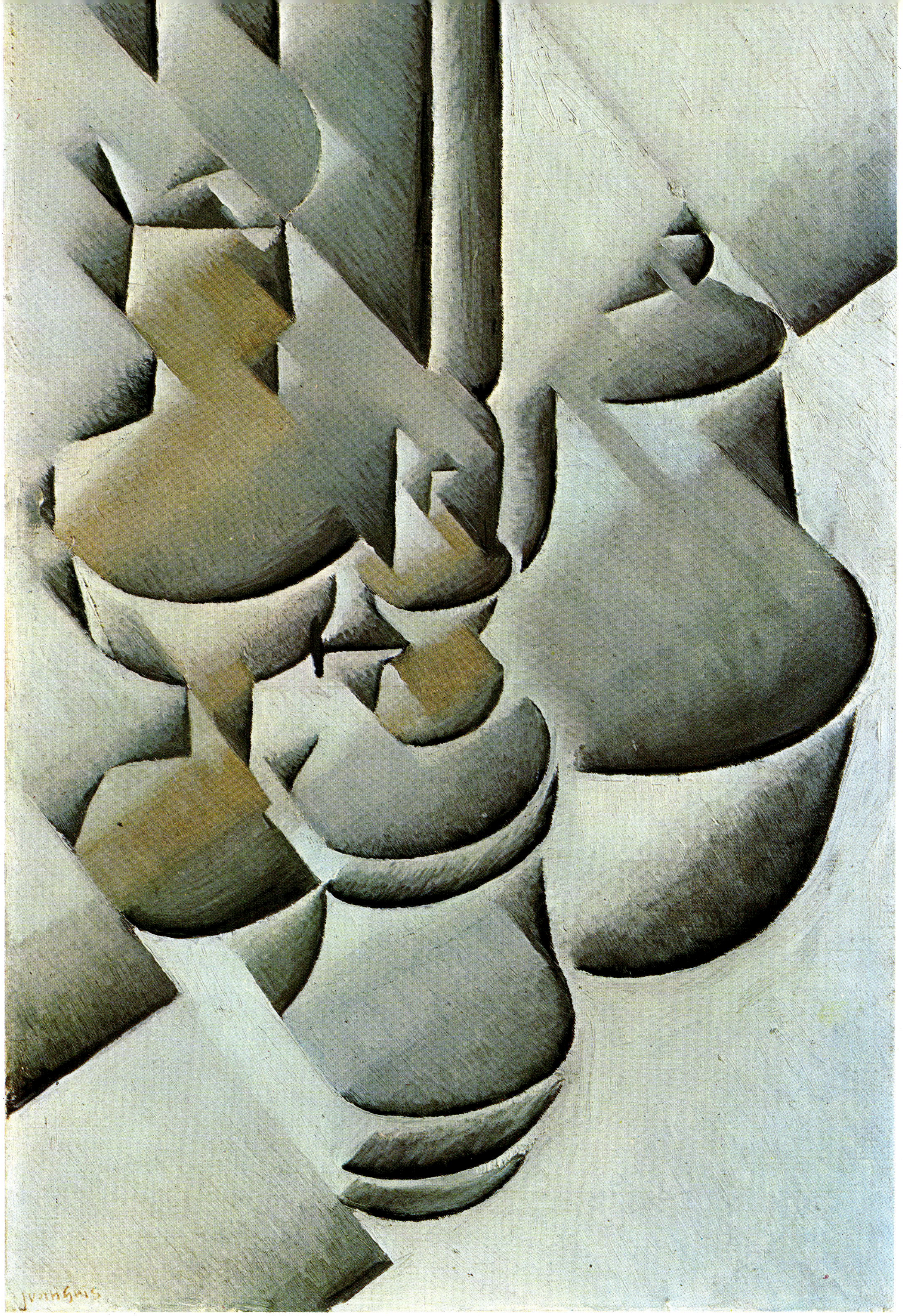

Juan Gris: *Still Life with Oil Lamp, 1912*

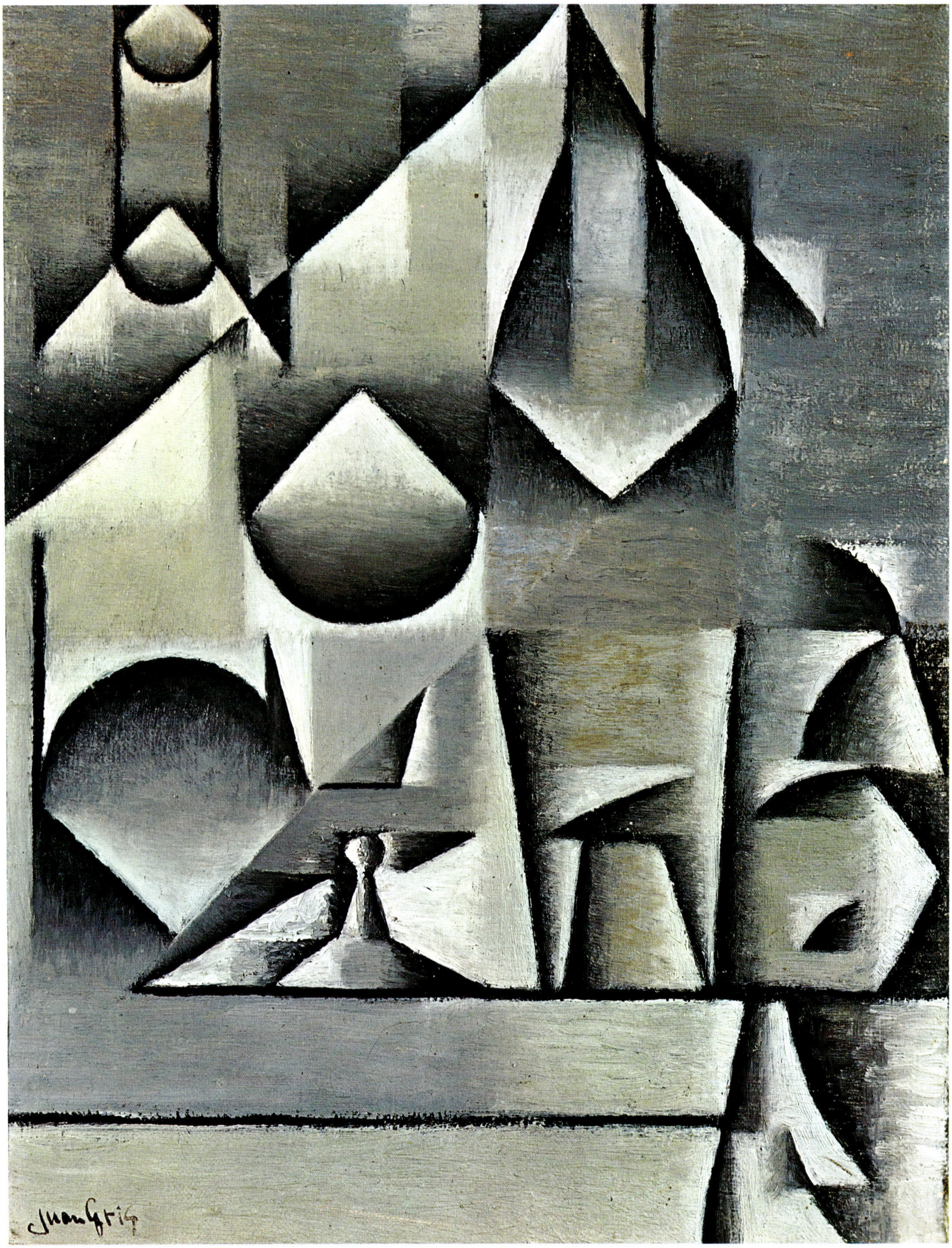

 Juan Gris: *Grey Still Life*, 1912

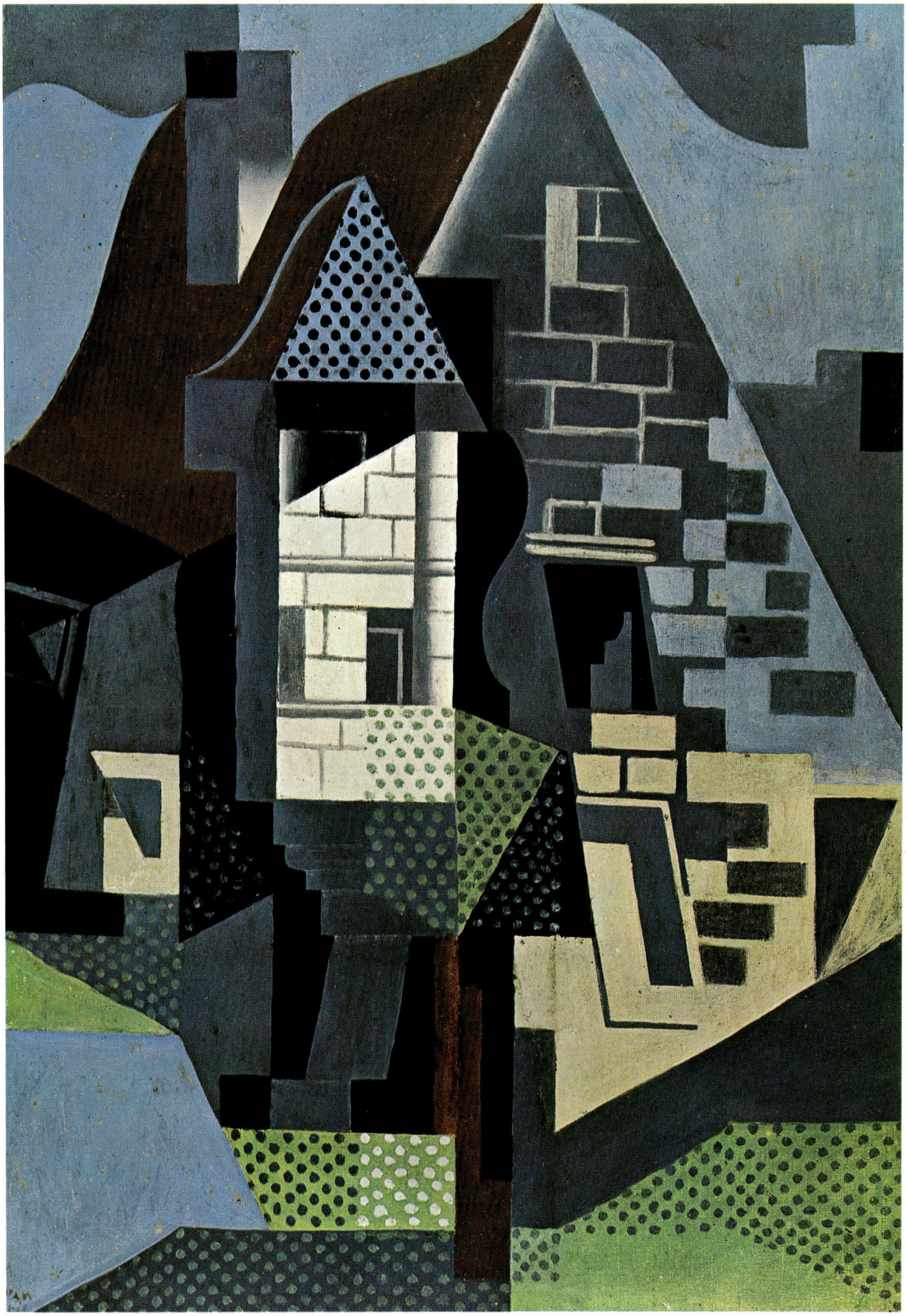

Juan Gris: *House in a Landscape (Beaulieu)*, 1918

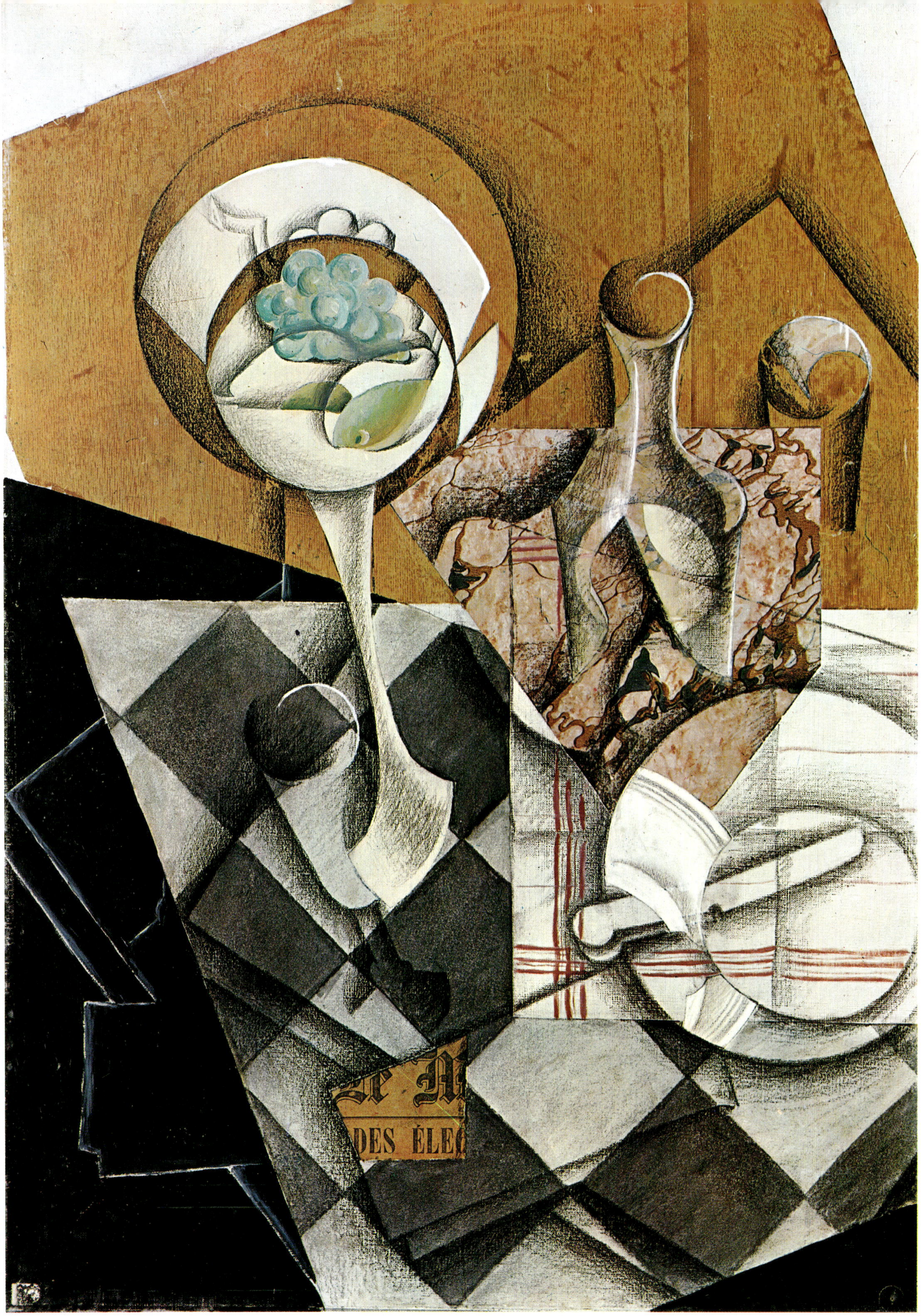

Juan Gris: *Still Life with Fruit Dish and Carafe*, 1914

Fernand Léger

Another, and again very different, expression of Cubism was in the work of Fernand Léger (1881-1955). He was fascinated by the mechanization of the modern world: machines were his inspiration. He wrote of his picture *Nude Figures in a Wood*, "I had an obsession. I was set on 'disjointing' bodies. You know what they called me - a 'Tubist'!" Soon the idea of "contrasts of forms" seized him. *Woman in Blue* opposed his usual small tubes with larger, flat shapes. Like other Cubists, he included realistically depicted objects in abstract paintings: in this case there is a recognizable section of table and vase in the picture's center right. The cannons he encountered in World War I are said to have emphasized his previous interest in the cylindrical: *Woman in Red and Green* and *Soldier with Pipe* demonstrate their impact

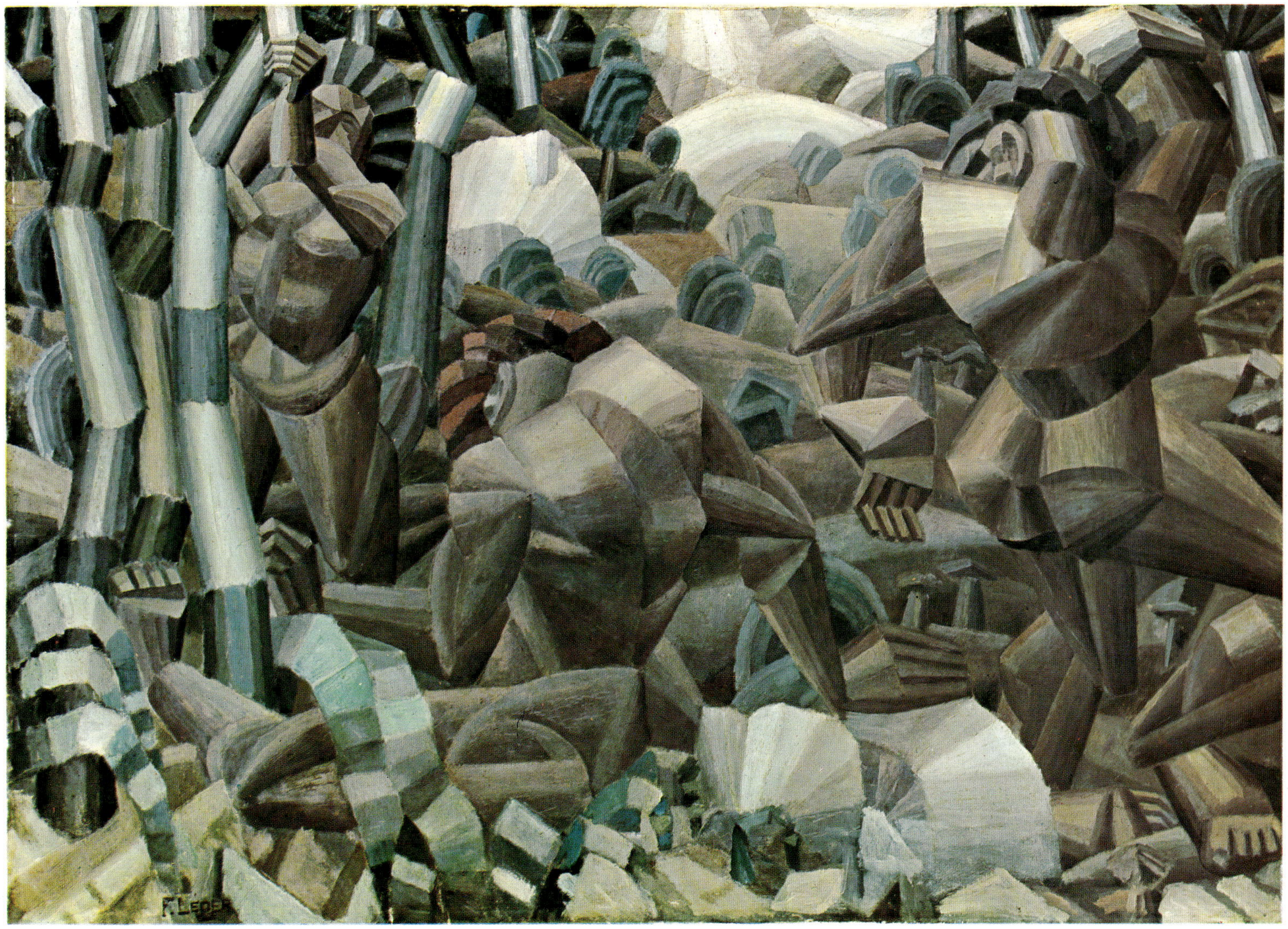

Fernand Léger: *Nude Figures in a Wood,* 1909-1911

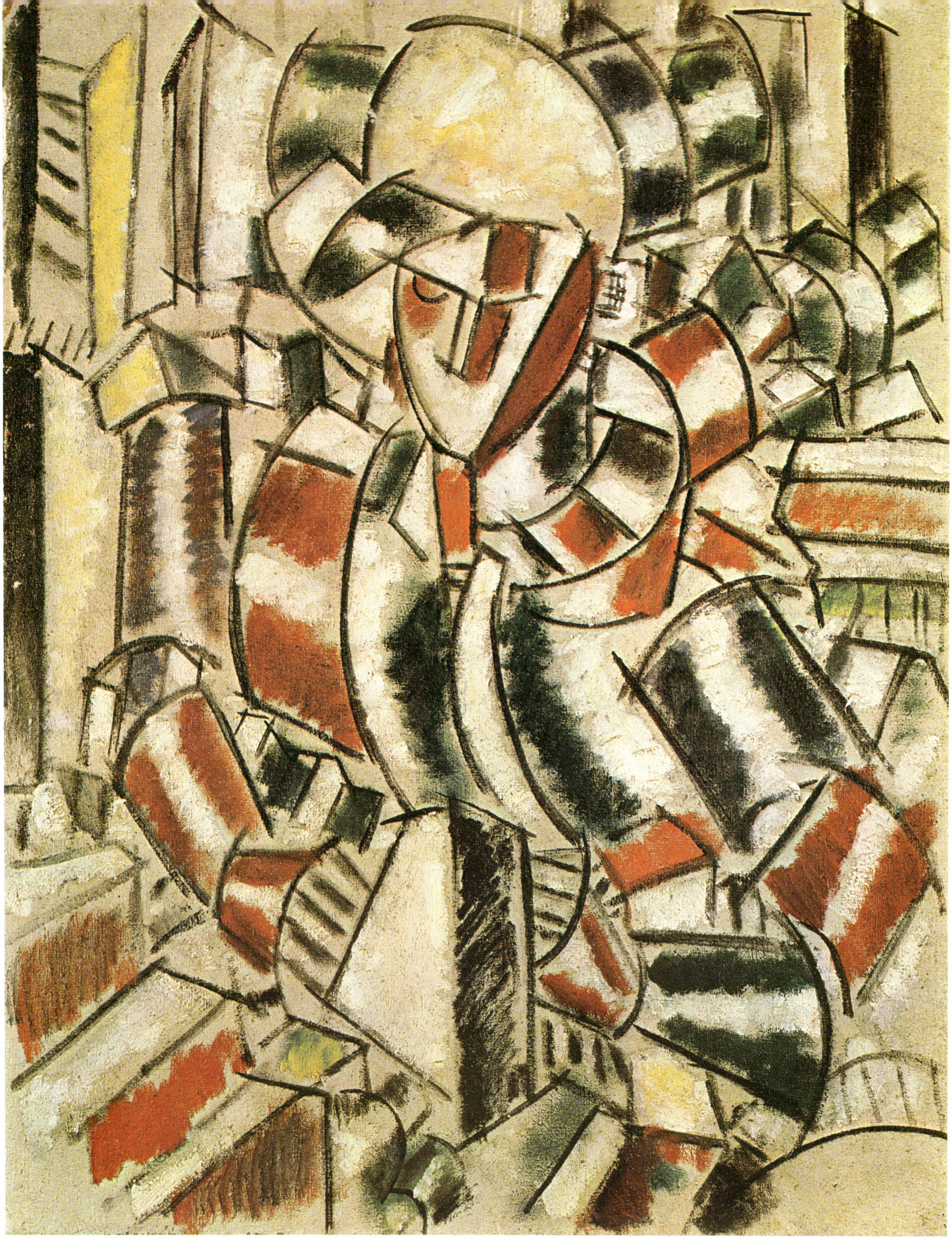

Fernand Léger: *Woman in Red and Green*, 1914

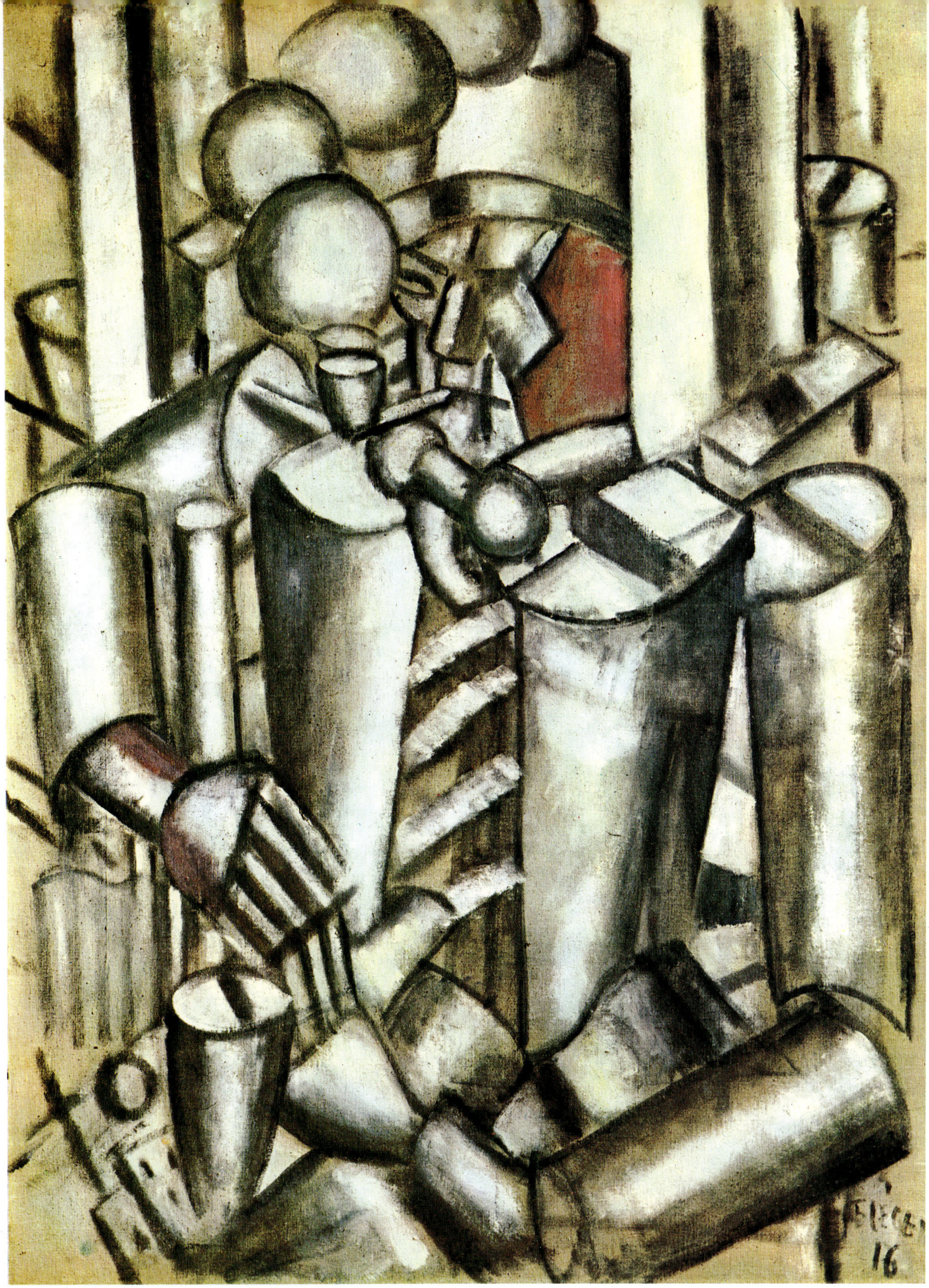

Fernand Léger: *Soldier with Pipe,* 1916

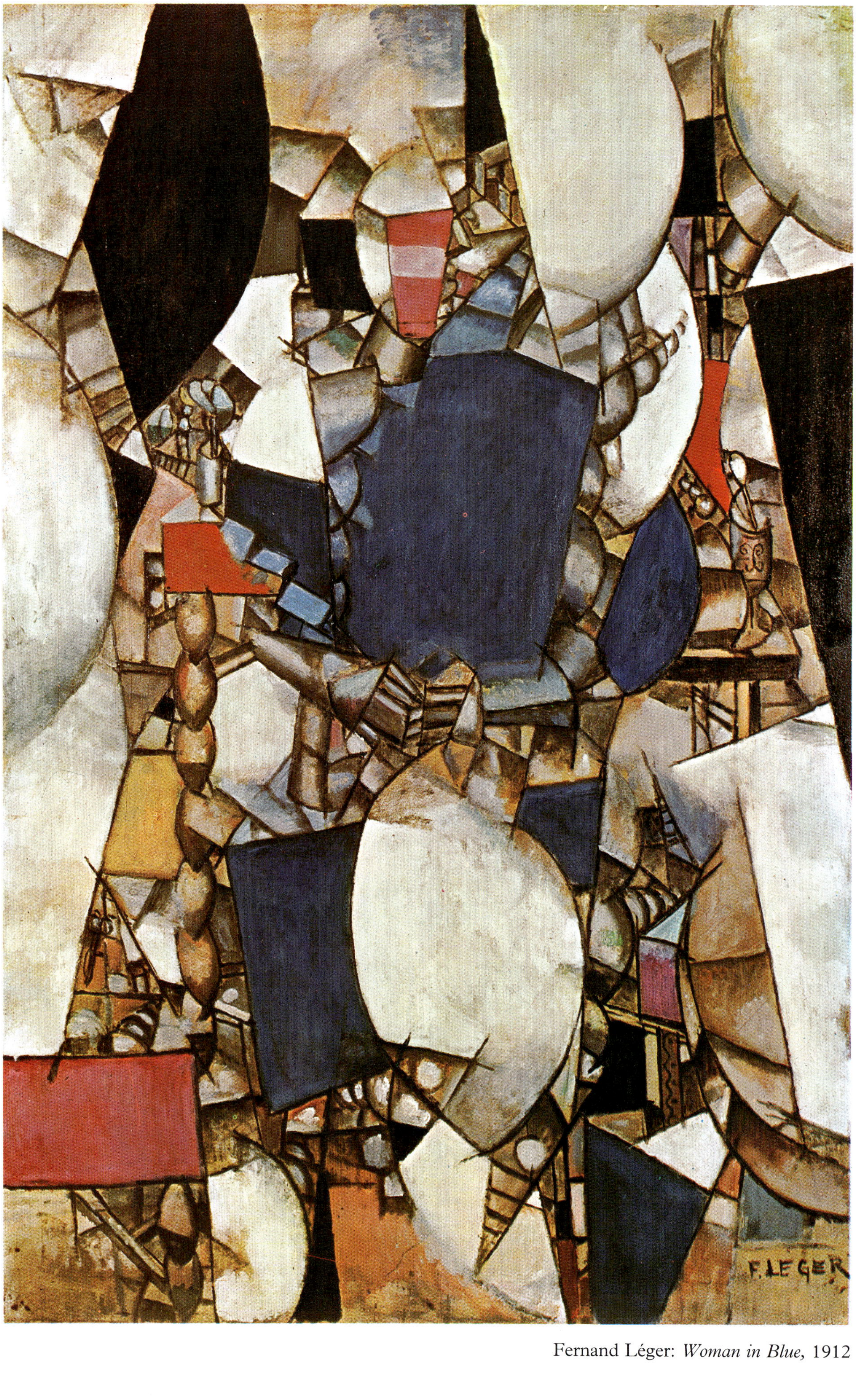

Fernand Léger: *Woman in Blue,* 1912

Robert Delaunay

Two early Cubist paintings by Robert Delaunay (1885-1941), *The Eiffel Tower* and *The City* attracted extreme hostility when exhibited at the Salon des Artistes Indépendants in 1911. (Picasso and Braque still refused to exhibit there, showing their work at their dealers' galleries.) One critic said of the first picture that it was "an Eiffel Tower toppled over, presumably with an eye to destoying the nearby houses which, dancing a cancan, are rudely sticking their chimney pots into each other's windows."

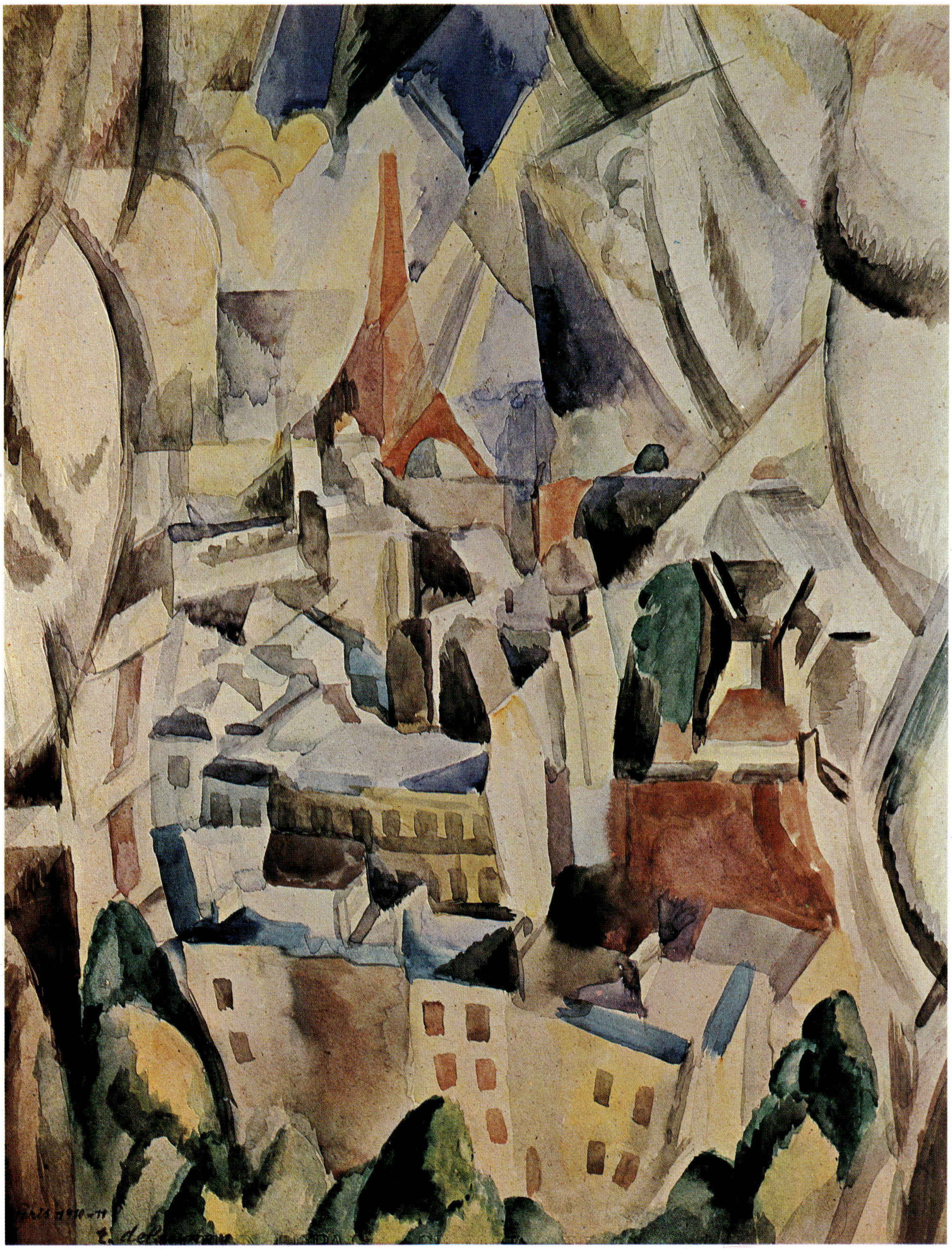

Robert Delaunay: *The Eiffel Tower,* 1910-1911

Delaunay was greatly interested in light and what it did to objects, such as buildings, and their planes. His interpretation of light's disintegrative effects in paintings such as these two was called "catastrophic art", a term which he did not reject.

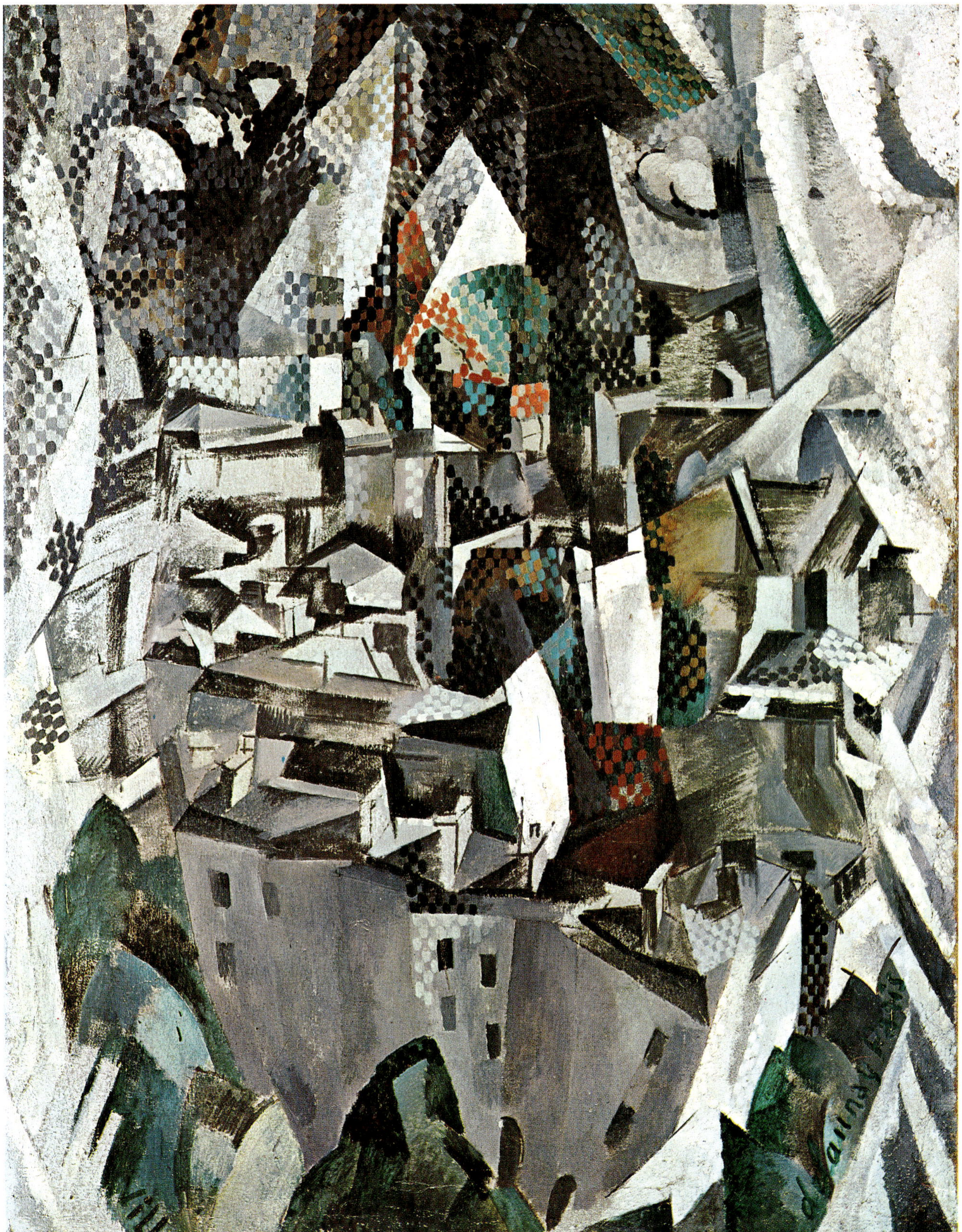

Robert Delaunay: *The City, No 2.* 1910

Jacques Villon and Marcel Duchamp

Jacques Villon (1875-1963) was born Gaston Duchamp, brother of the artists Marcel and Raymond, who introduced him to Cubism. Cubist influence is evident in his *Portrait of Raymond Duchamp-Villon.* His interest in line in rhythm, "the line of the vital urge in all things", as he described it, rather than in color, is obvious in *Soldiers on the March.* The fascination with movement links him to the Futurists, an Italian artistic group that believed "everything moves, all is in a state of flux..."

Another "Cubist-Futurist", Villon's brother, Marcel Duchamp (1887-1968), caused a major scandal (though also a publicity triumph) at the Armory Show in New York in 1913 with his *Nude Descending a Staircase, No. 2,* which was dubbed "an explosion in a shingle factory."

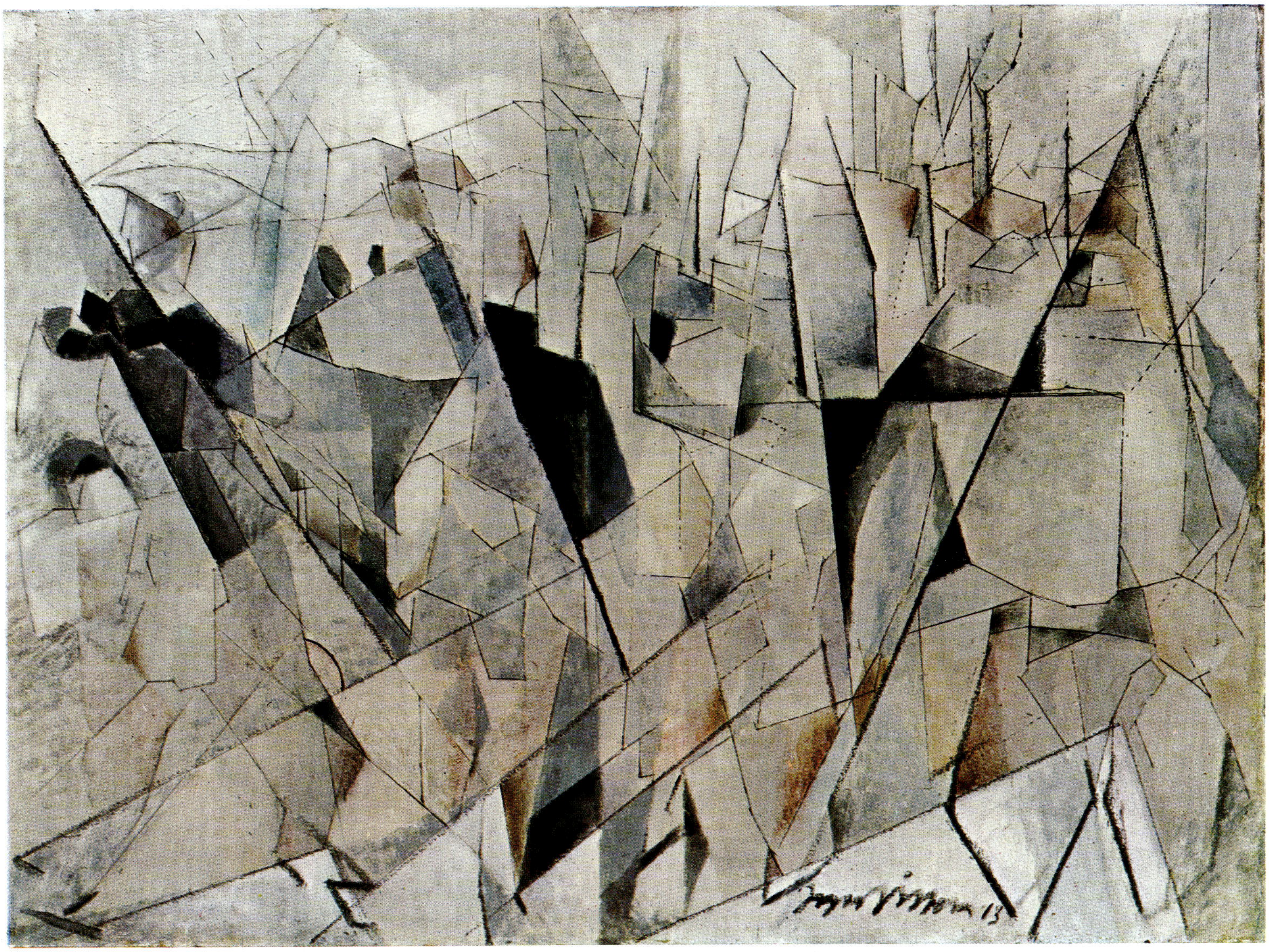

Jacques Villon: *Soldiers on the March,* 1913

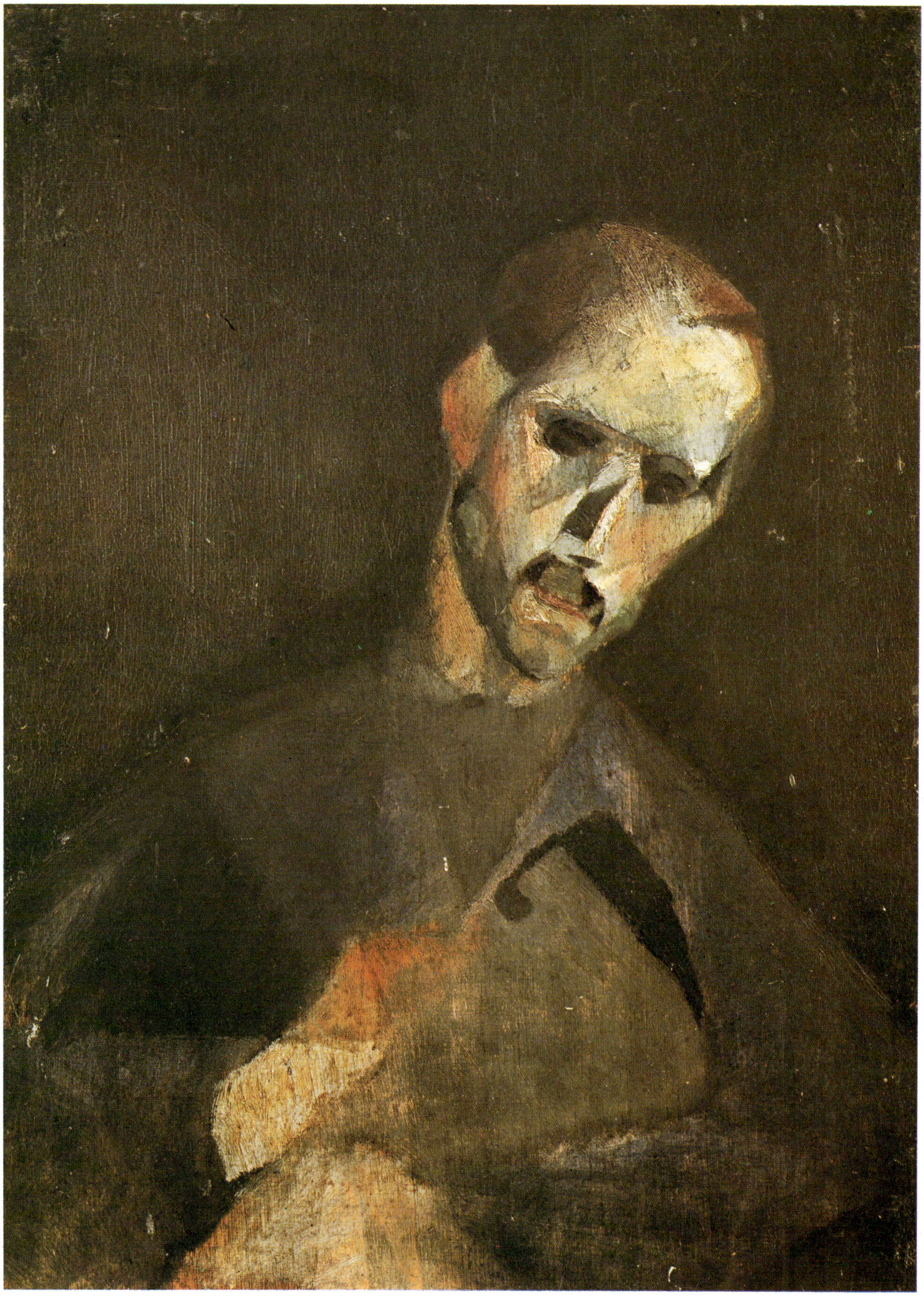

Jacques Villon: *Portait of Raymond Duchamp-Villon*, 1911

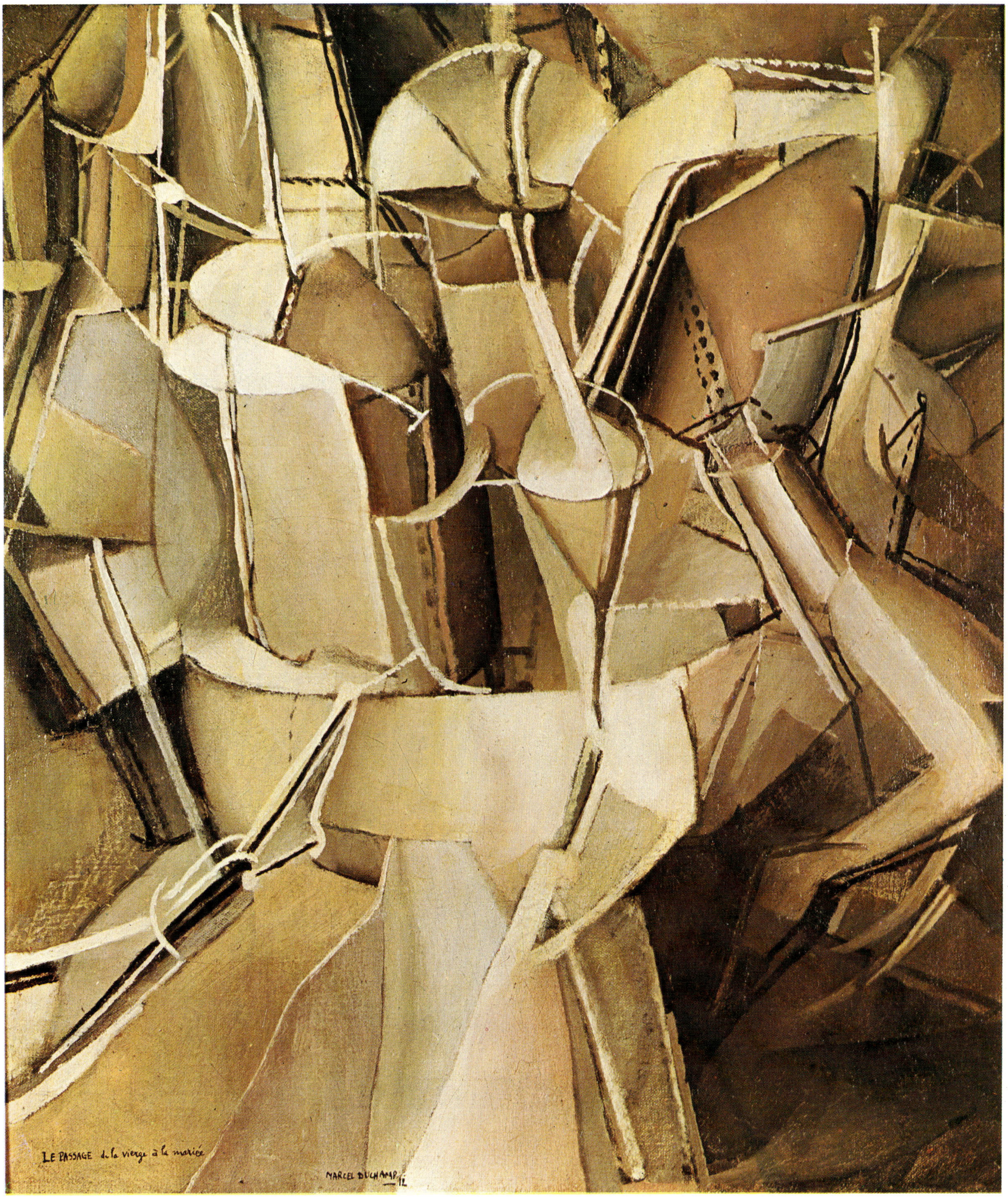

Marcel Duchamp: *Le Passage de la Vierge a la Mariee*, 1912

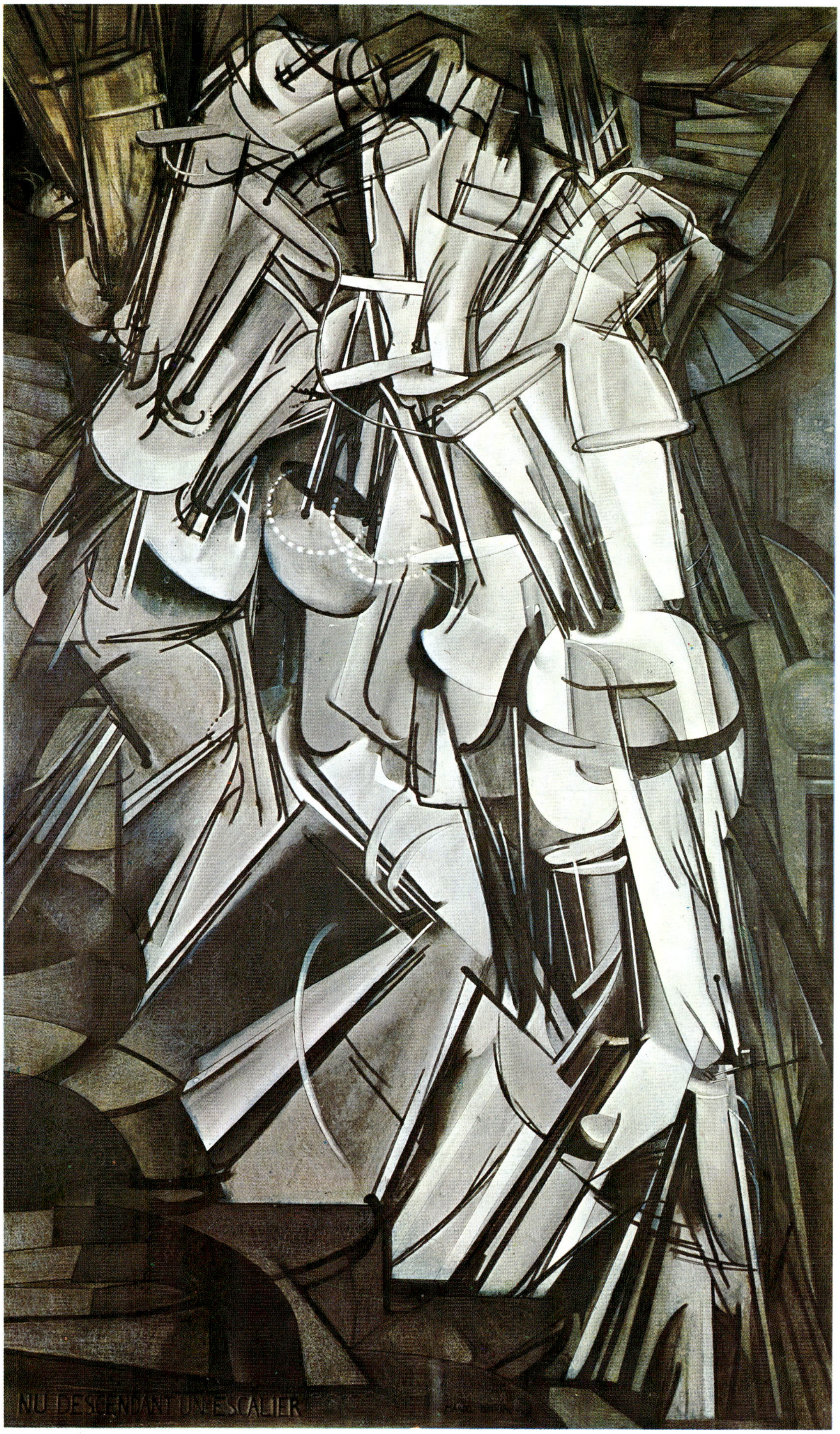

Marcel Duchamp: *Nude Descending a Staircase, No. 3,* 1916

André Derain

As with any artistic movement, the major luminaries of Cubism were surrounded by a constellation of other painters working in sympathy, including, Herbin, Kupka, de La Fresnaye, and Le Fauconnier. Several others, such Gleizes, Lhote, Marcoussis, Metzinger, and Picabia, belonged to the Cubist offshoot, the Section d'Or ("Golden Mean"), which included Gris and Léger, but whose driving force was the brothers Villon and Duchamp.

Cubism is no longer outrageous, but many still do not appreciate it. Picasso himself said, "The fact that for a long time Cubism has not been understood and that even today there are people who cannot see anything in it means nothing. I do not read English, an English book is a blank book to me. This does not mean that the English language does not exist. Why should I blame anyone but myself if I cannot understand what I know nothing about?"

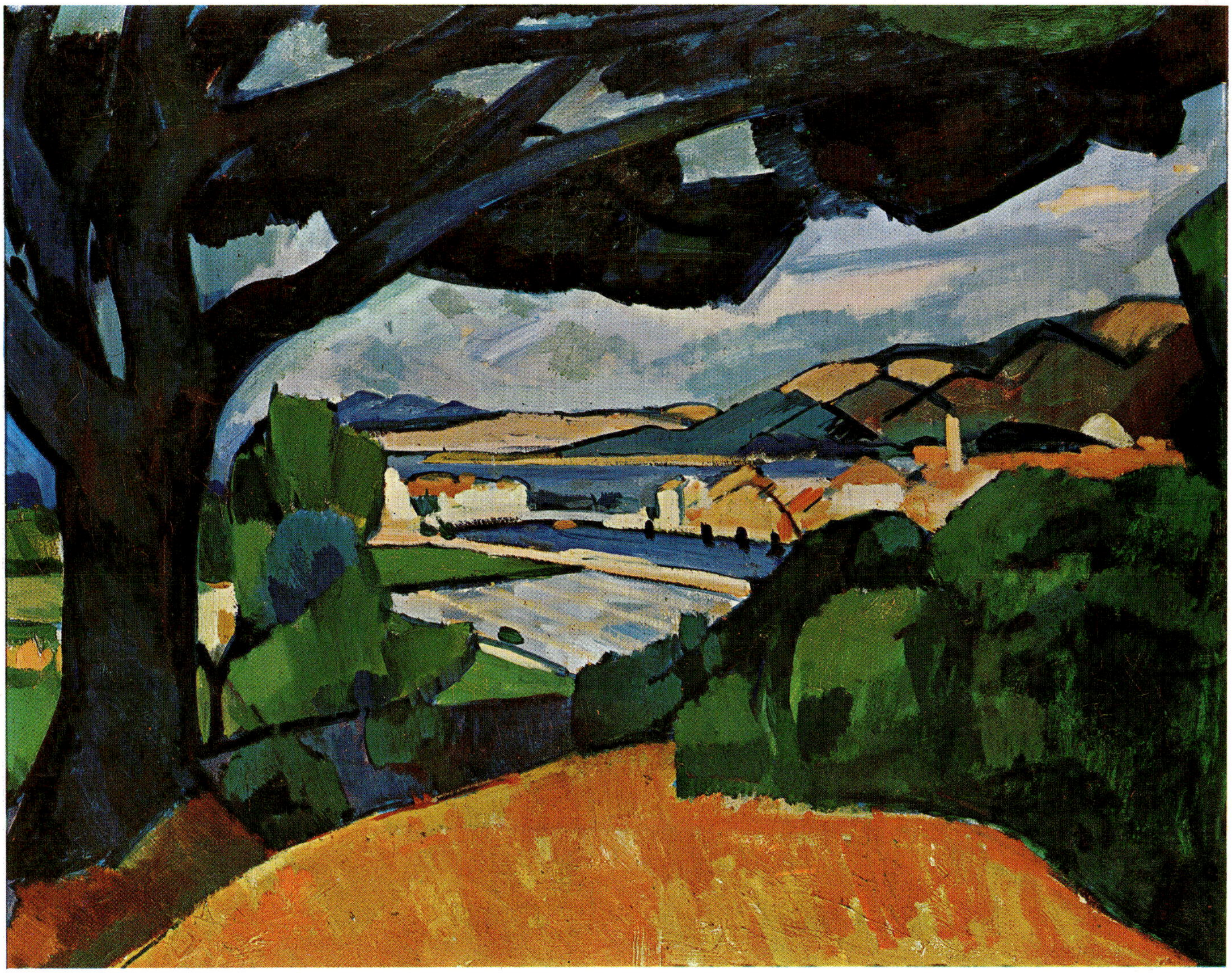

André Derain: *Martigues*, 1908

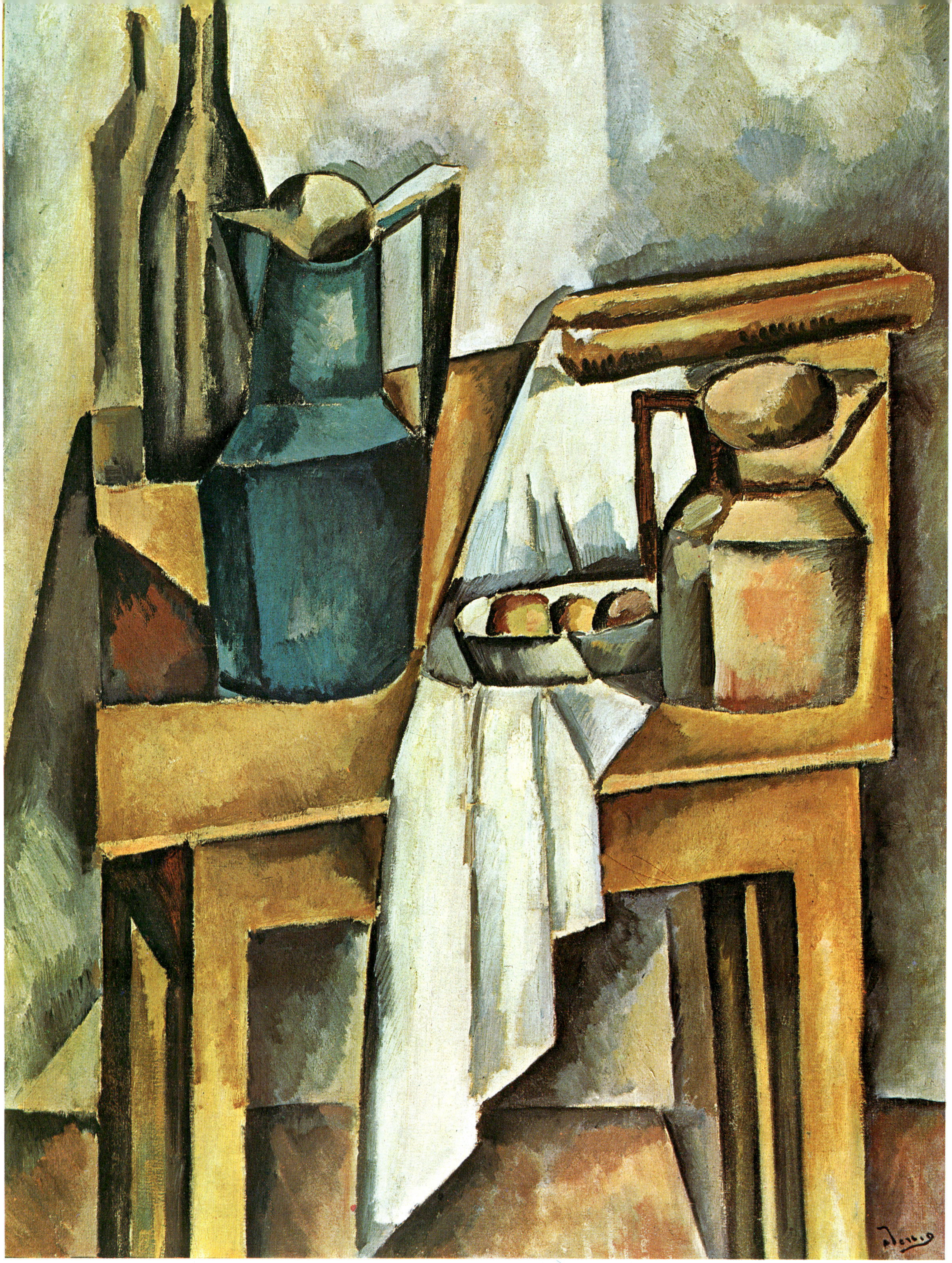

André Derain*: Still Life on a Table*, 1910

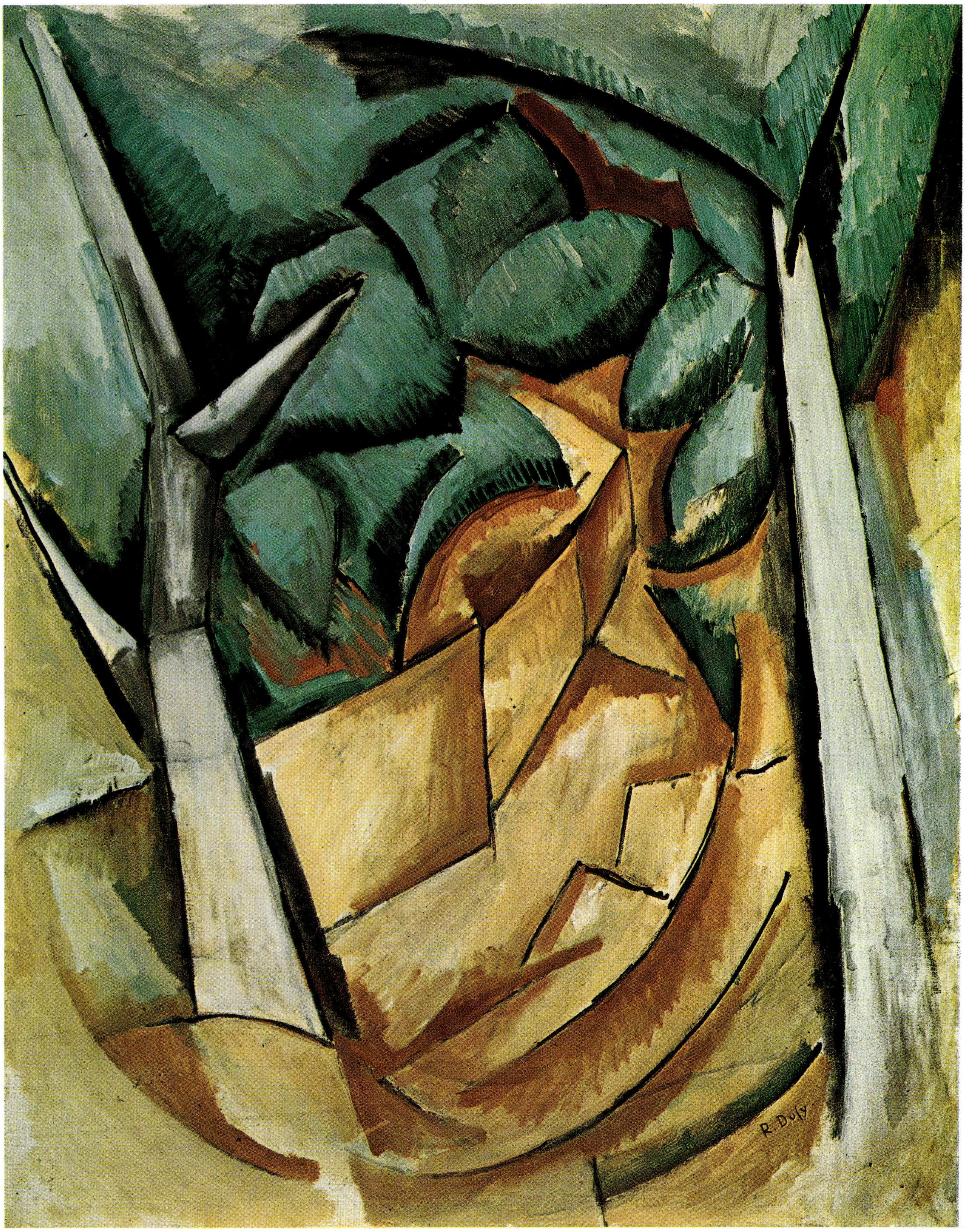

Raoul Dufy: *Landscape at L'Estaque,* 1908

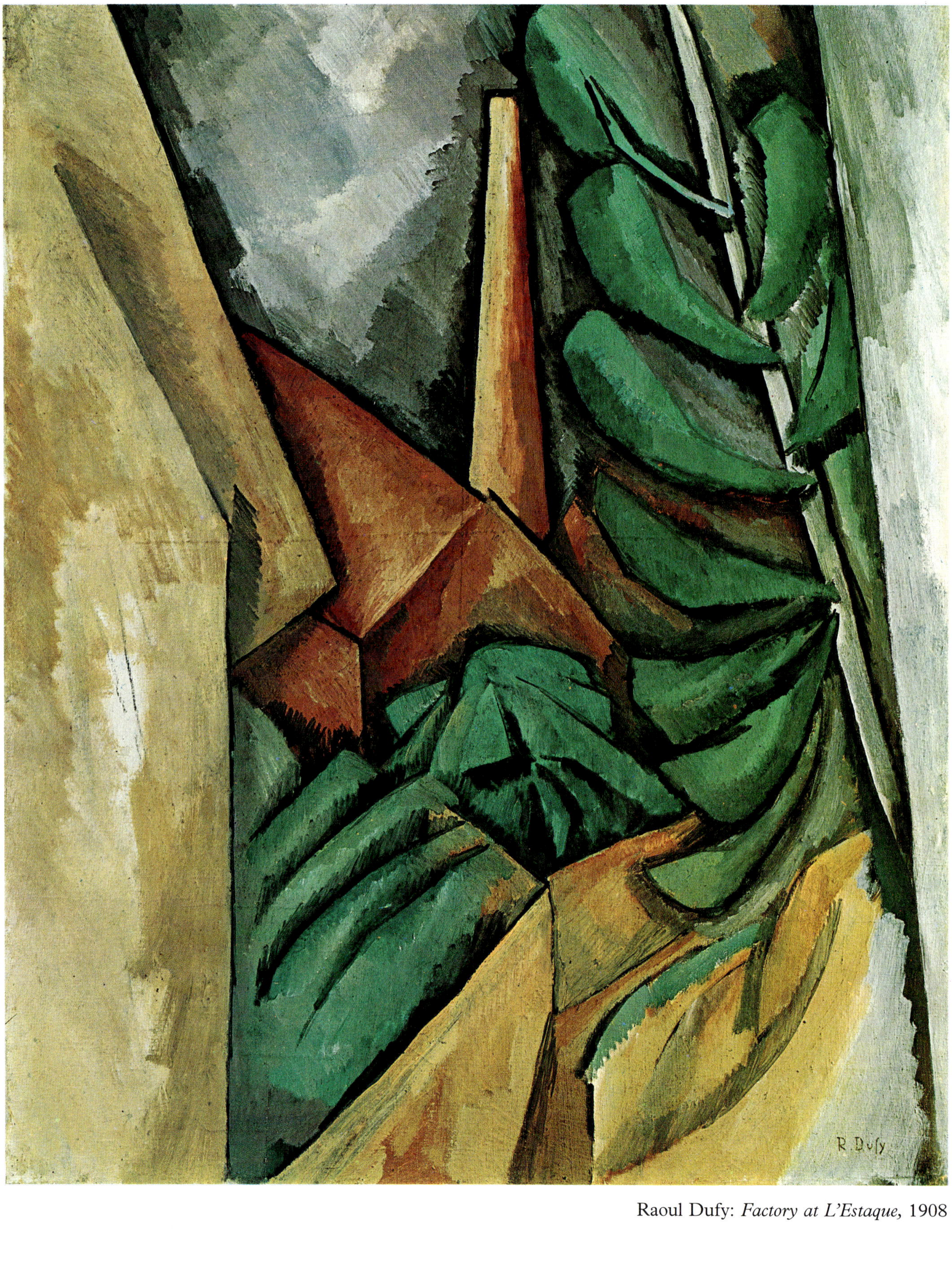

Raoul Dufy: *Factory at L'Estaque*, 1908

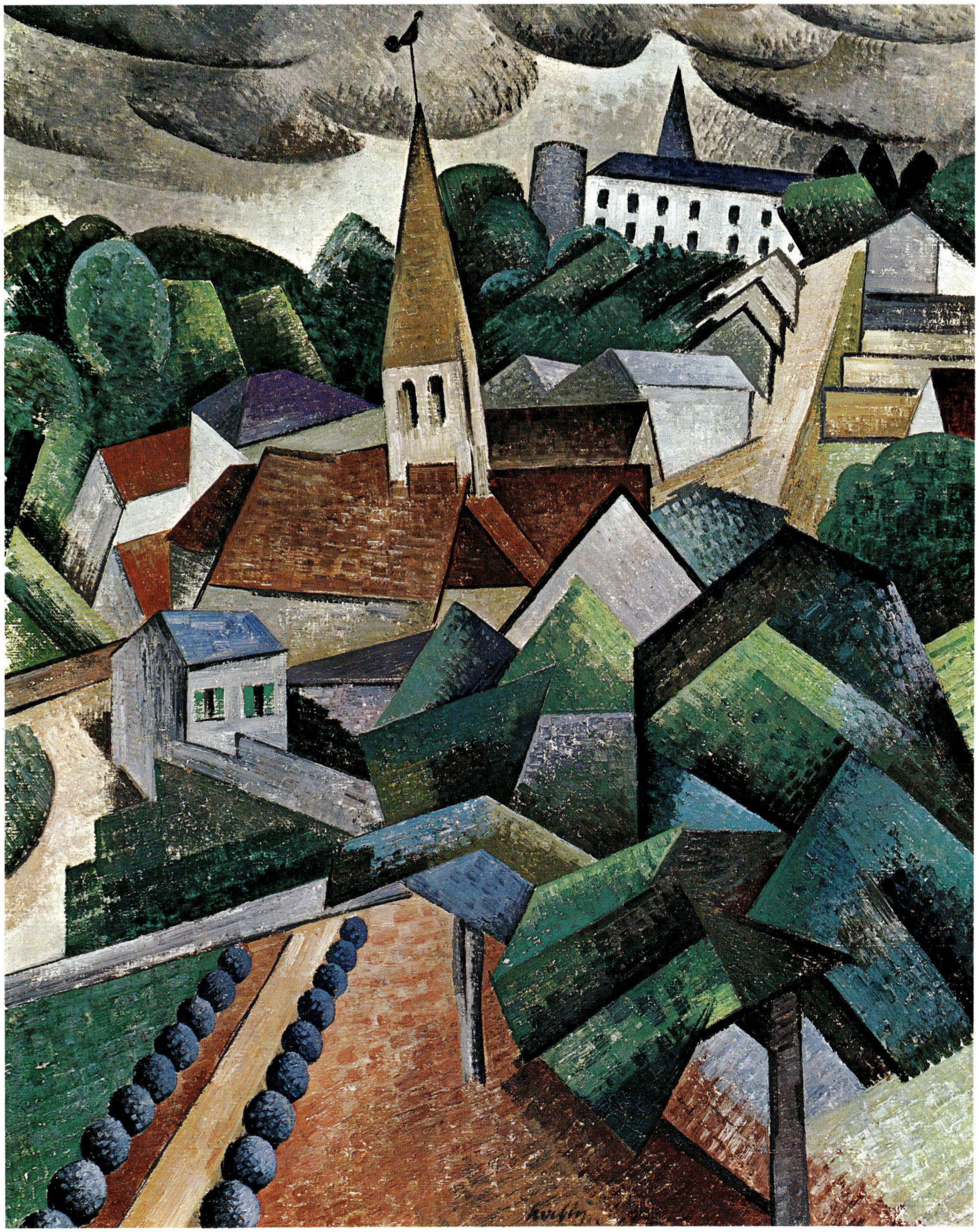

Auguste Herbin: *View of a Village on a Hillside,* 1911

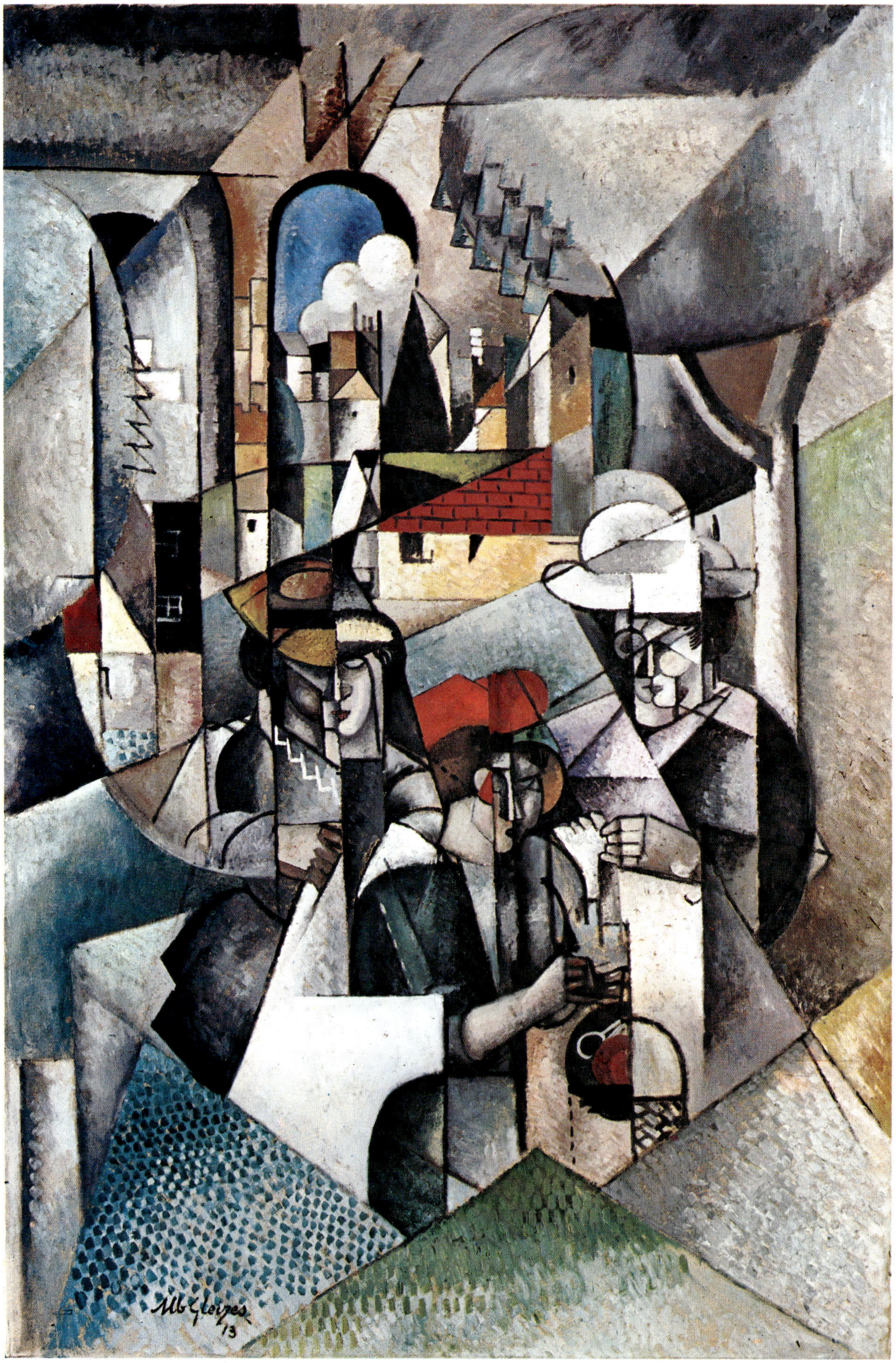

Albert Gleizes: *Woman Sewing*, 1913

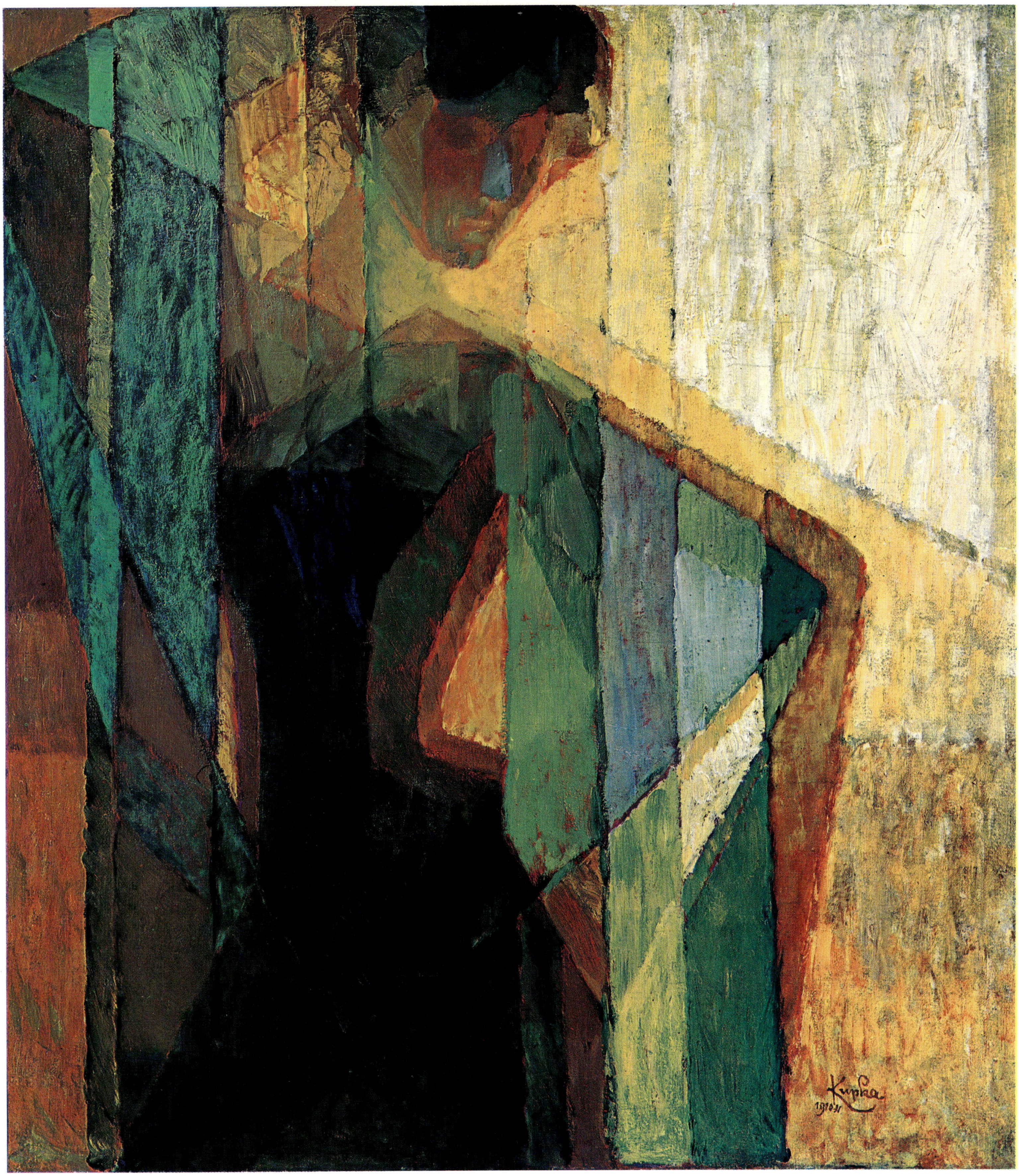

Frank Kupka: *Plans par Couleurs,* 1910–1911

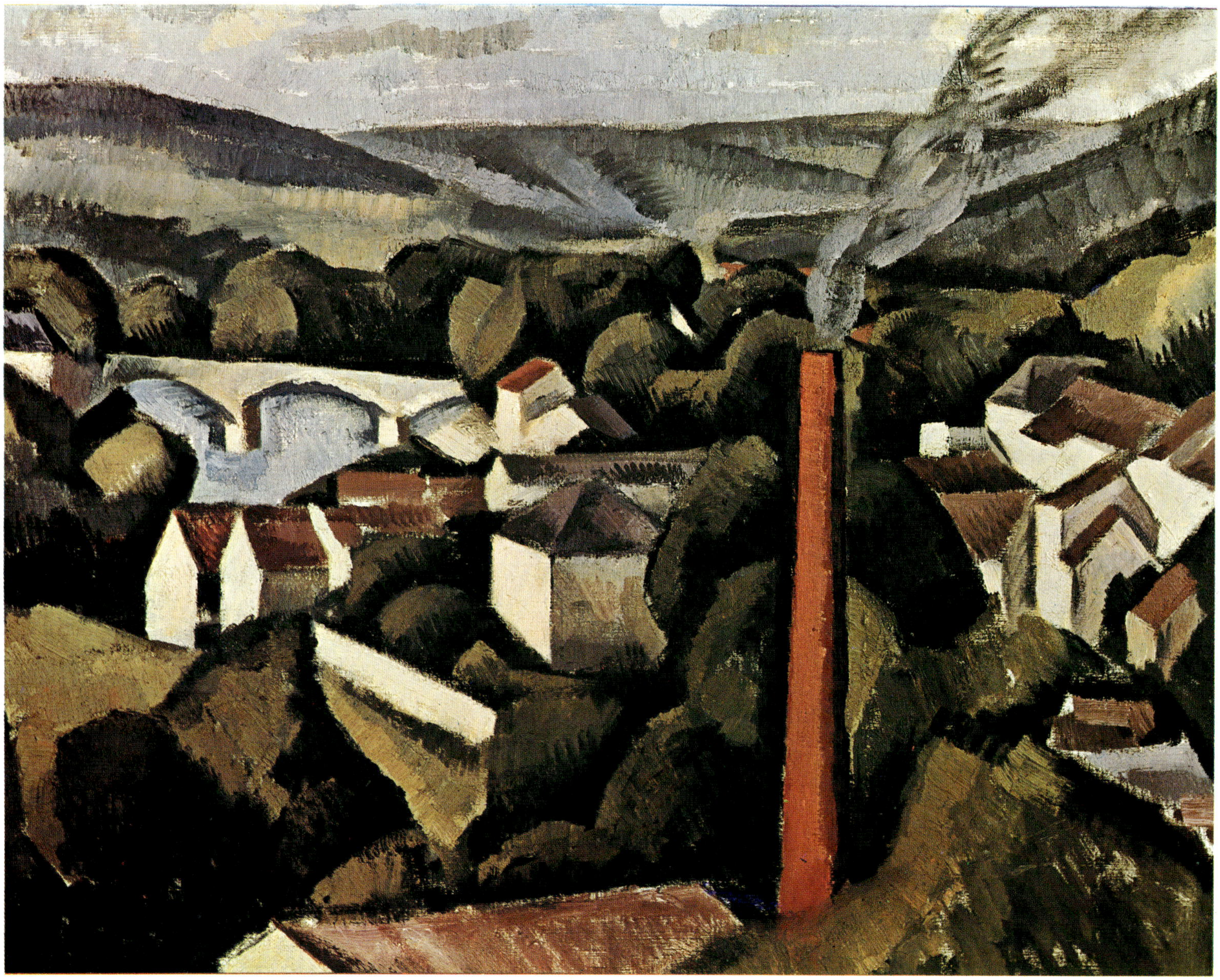

Roger de La Fresnaye: *Factory at La Ferté-sous-Jouarre,* 1911

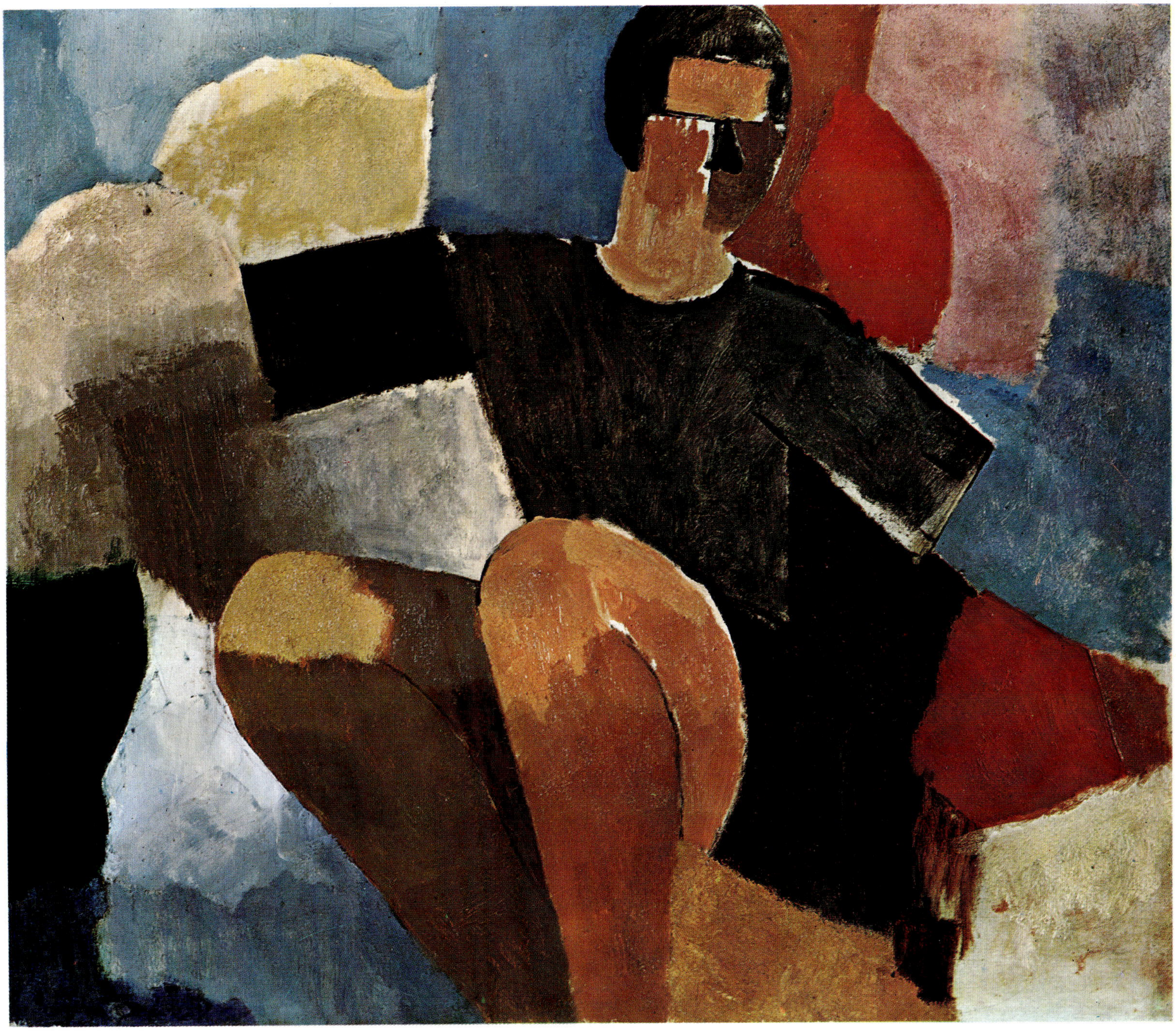

Roger de La Fresnaye: *The Rower,* 1914

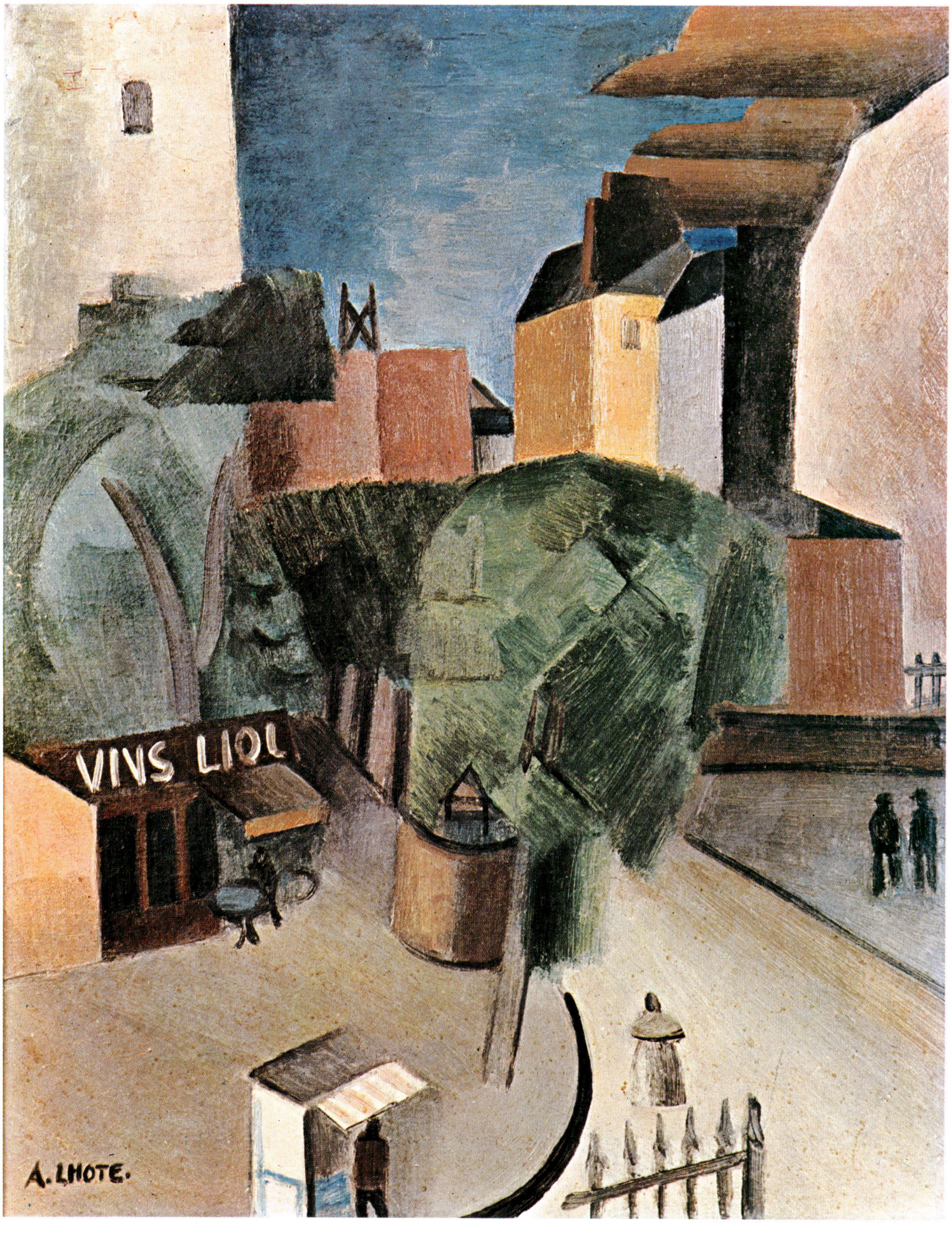

André Lhote: *Suburbs,* 1911

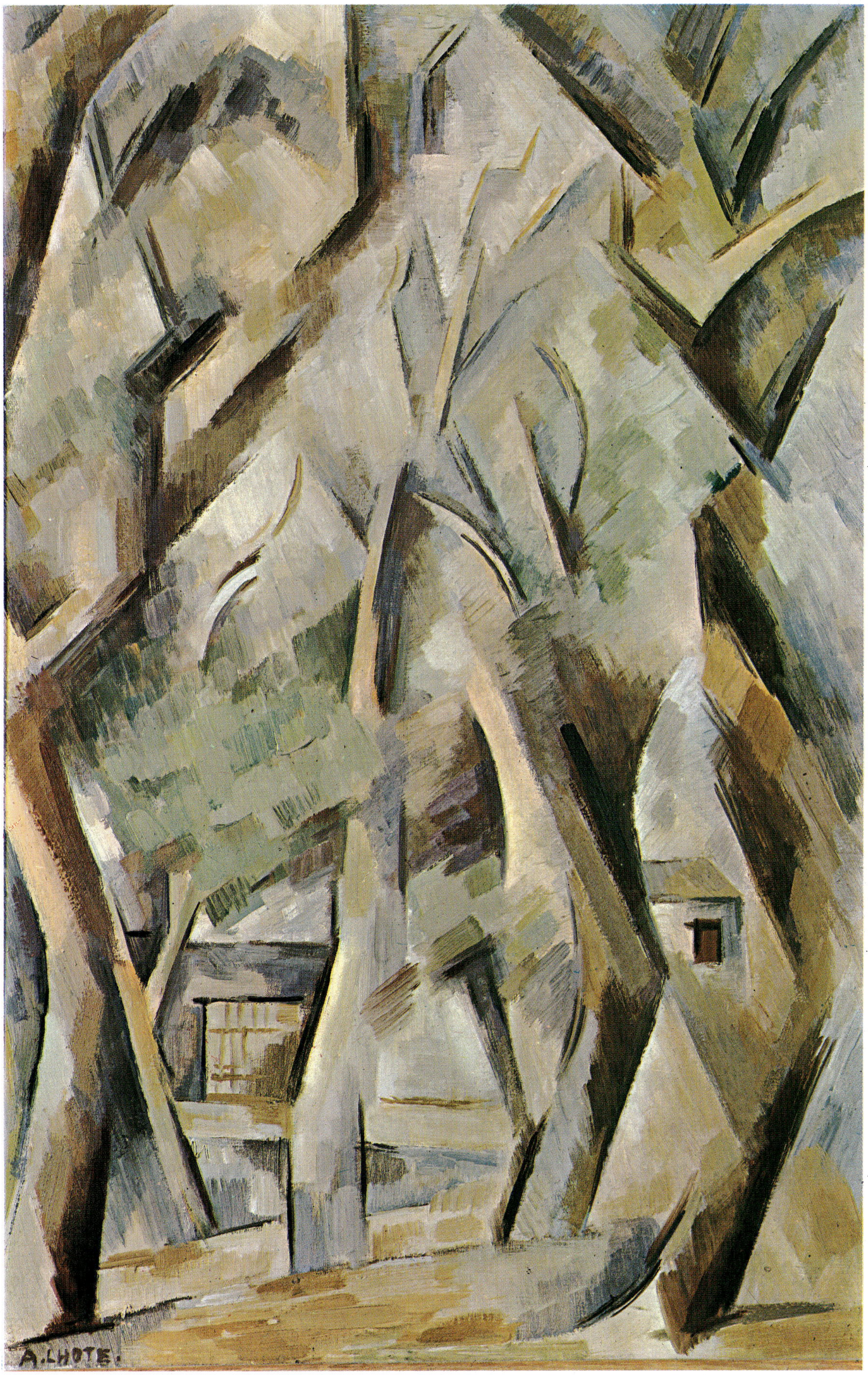

André Lhote: *Trees,* 1914

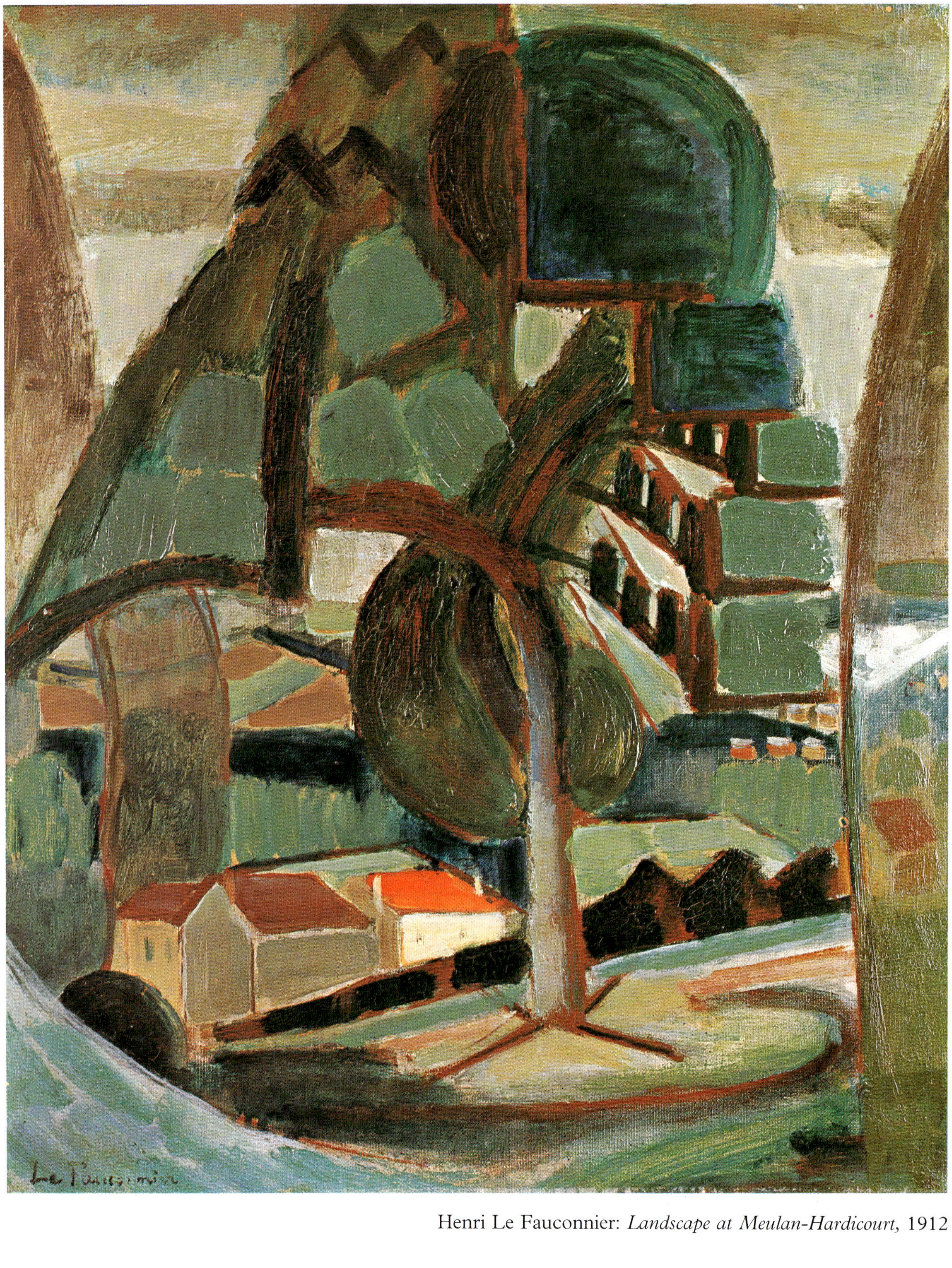

Henri Le Fauconnier: *Landscape at Meulan-Hardicourt*, 1912

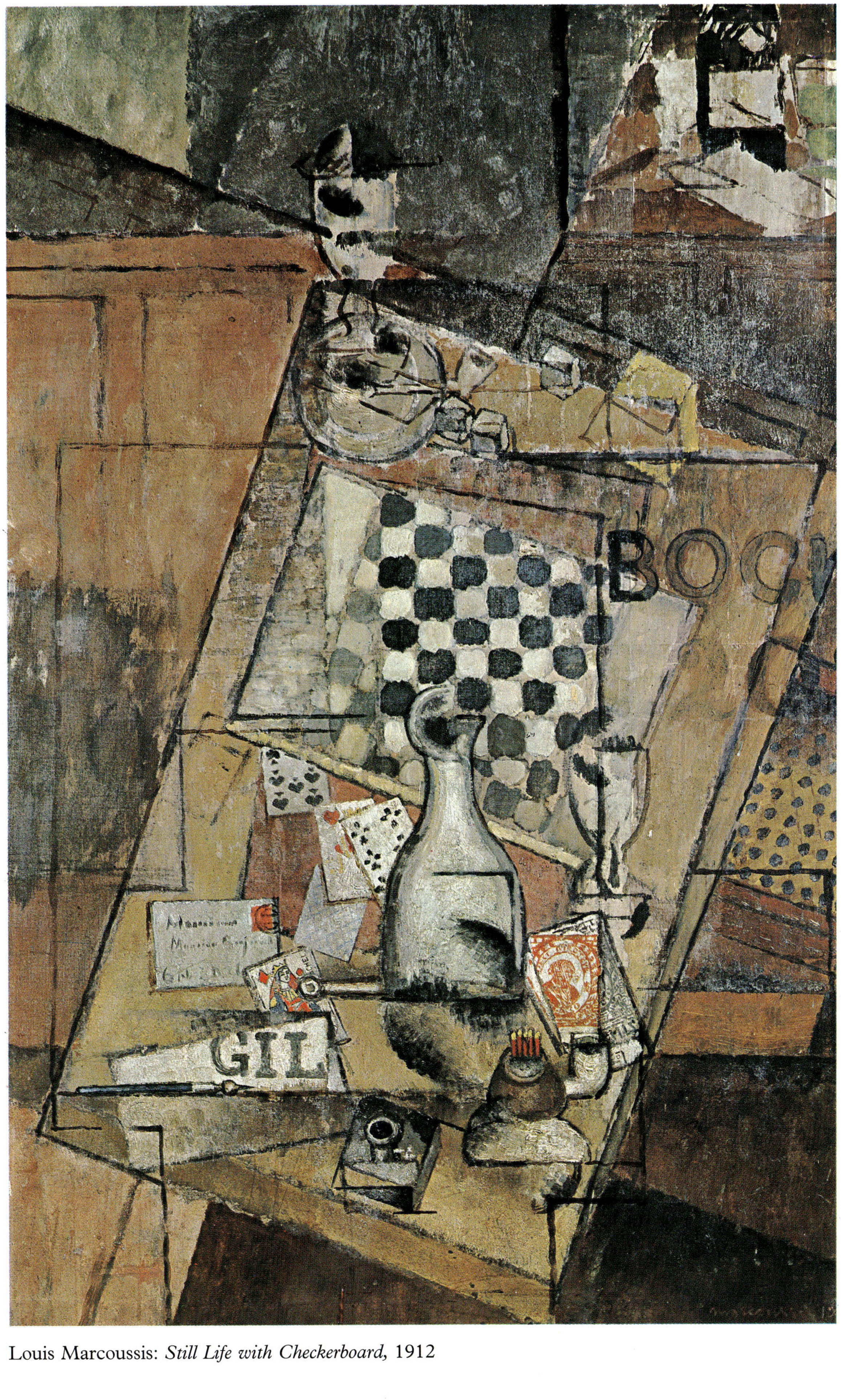

Louis Marcoussis: *Still Life with Checkerboard,* 1912

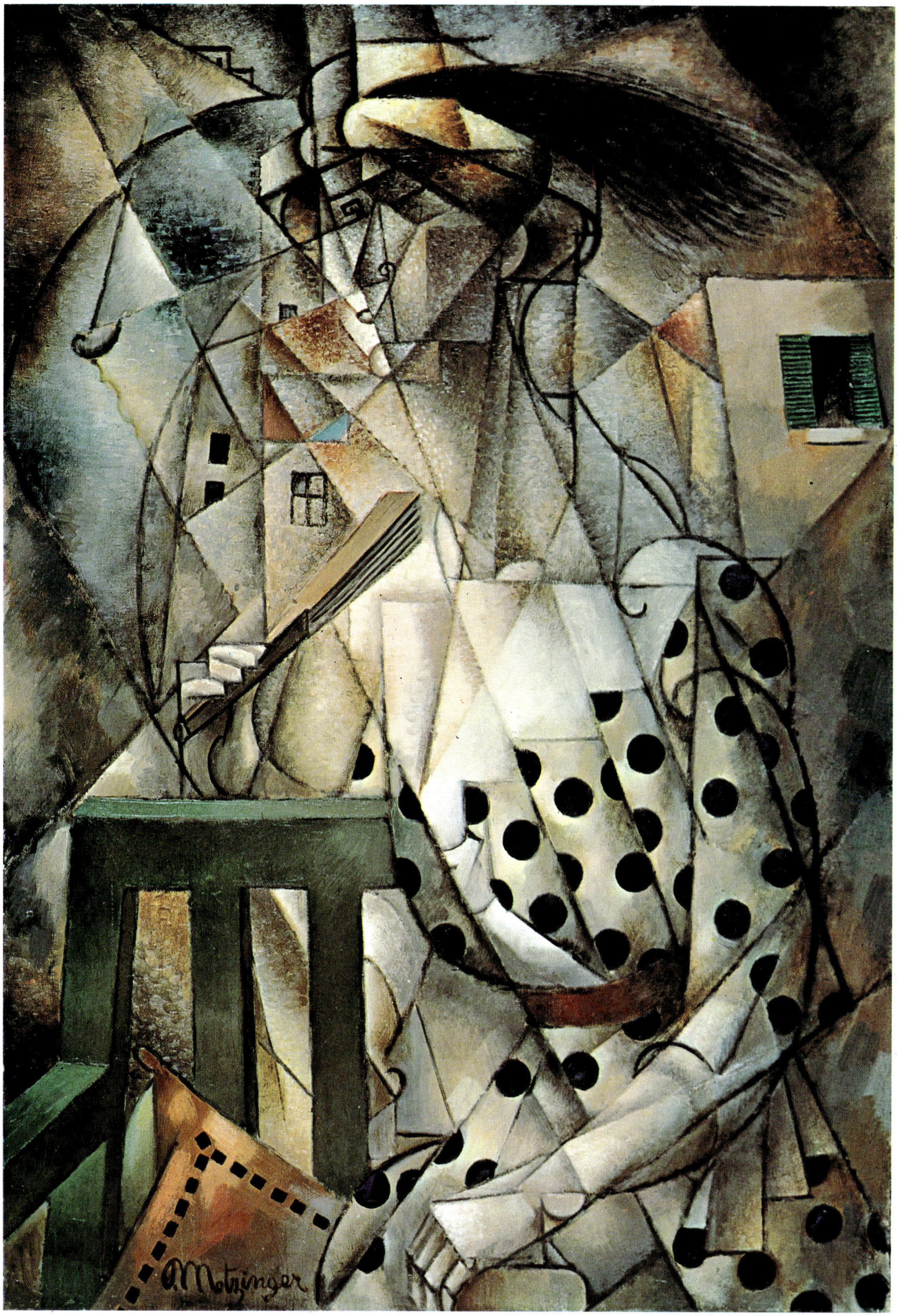

Jean Metzinger: *Woman with Fan,* 1913

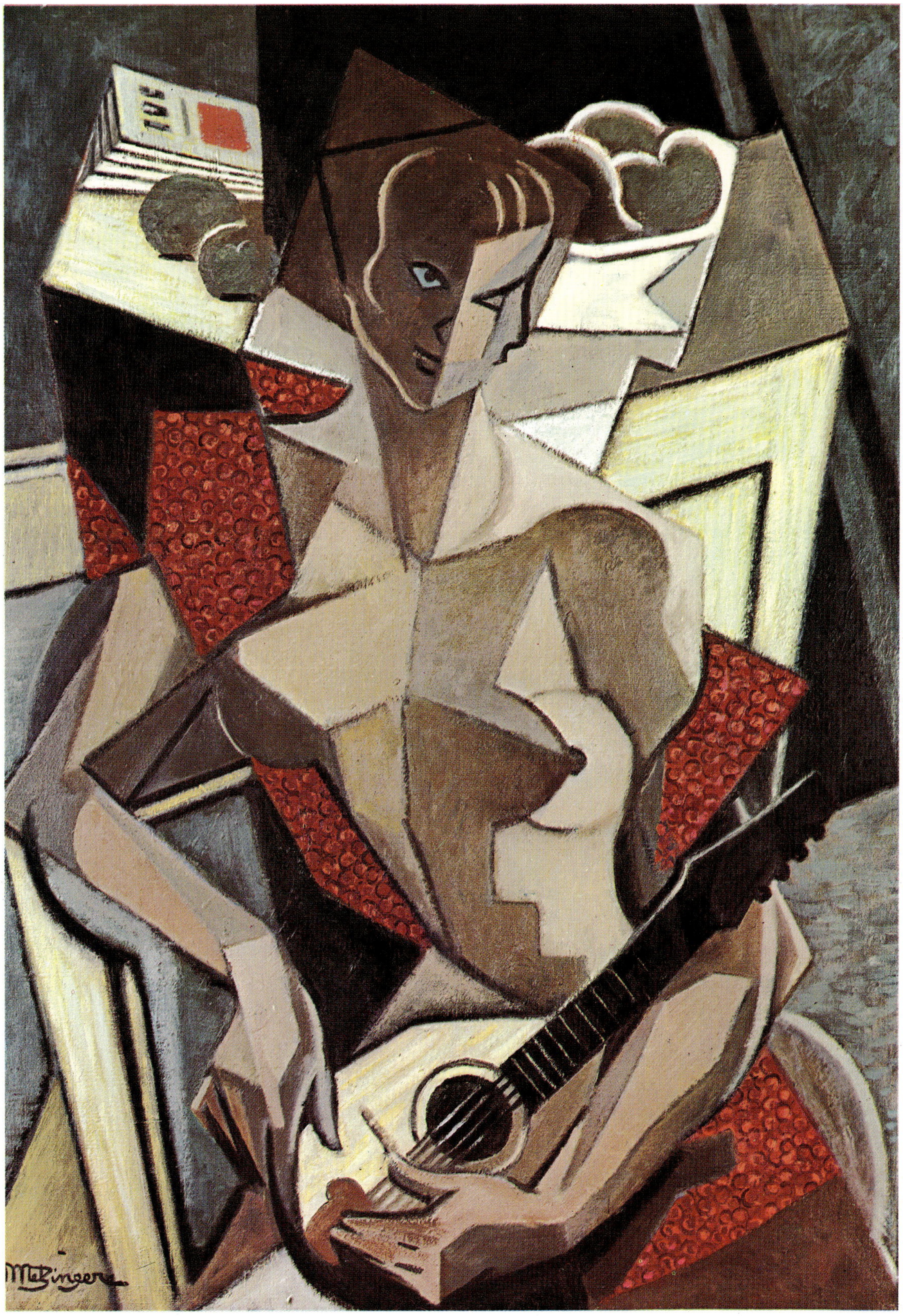

Jean Metzinger: *Woman with a Mandolin,* 1913

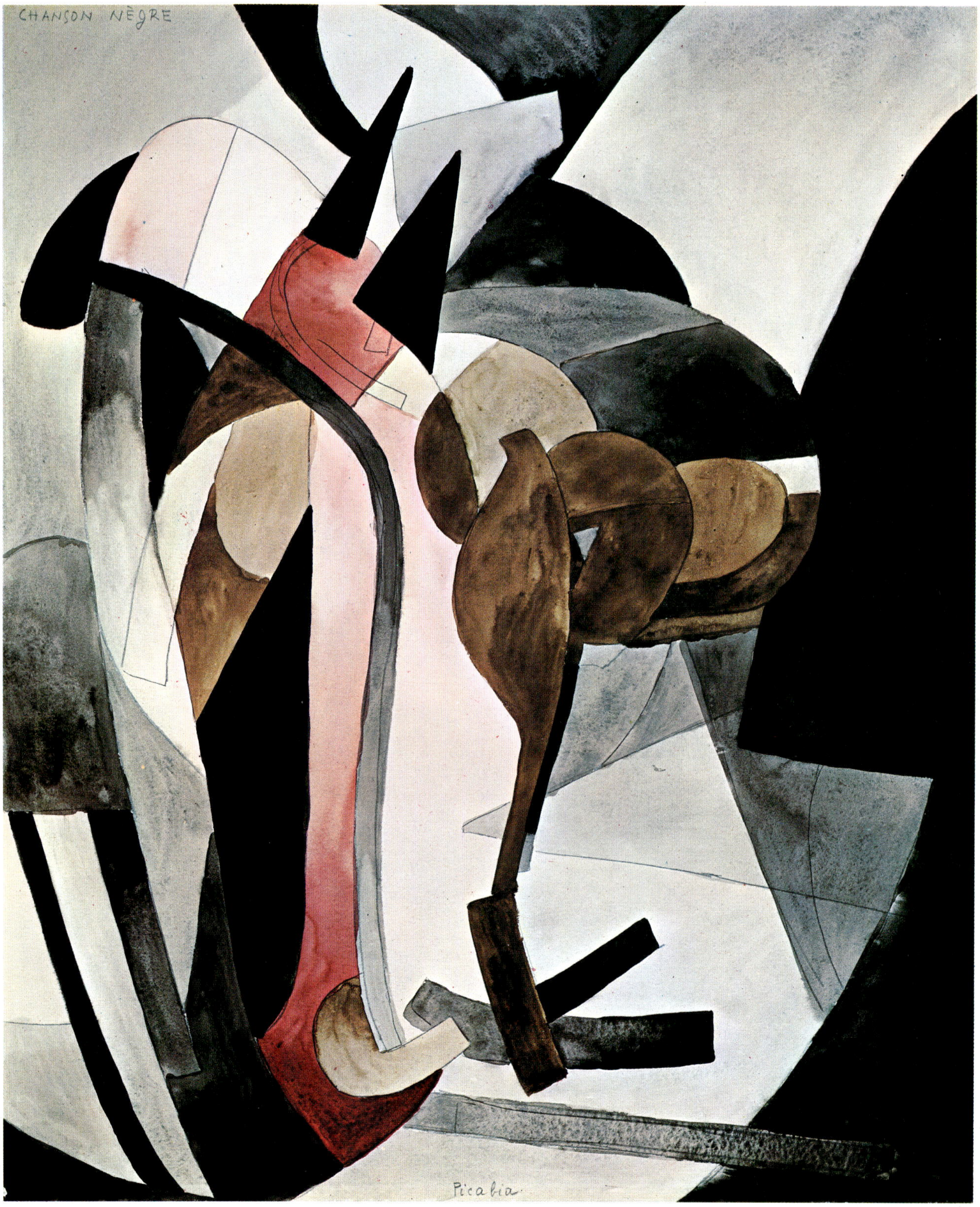

Francis Picabia: *Chanson Negré,* 1913

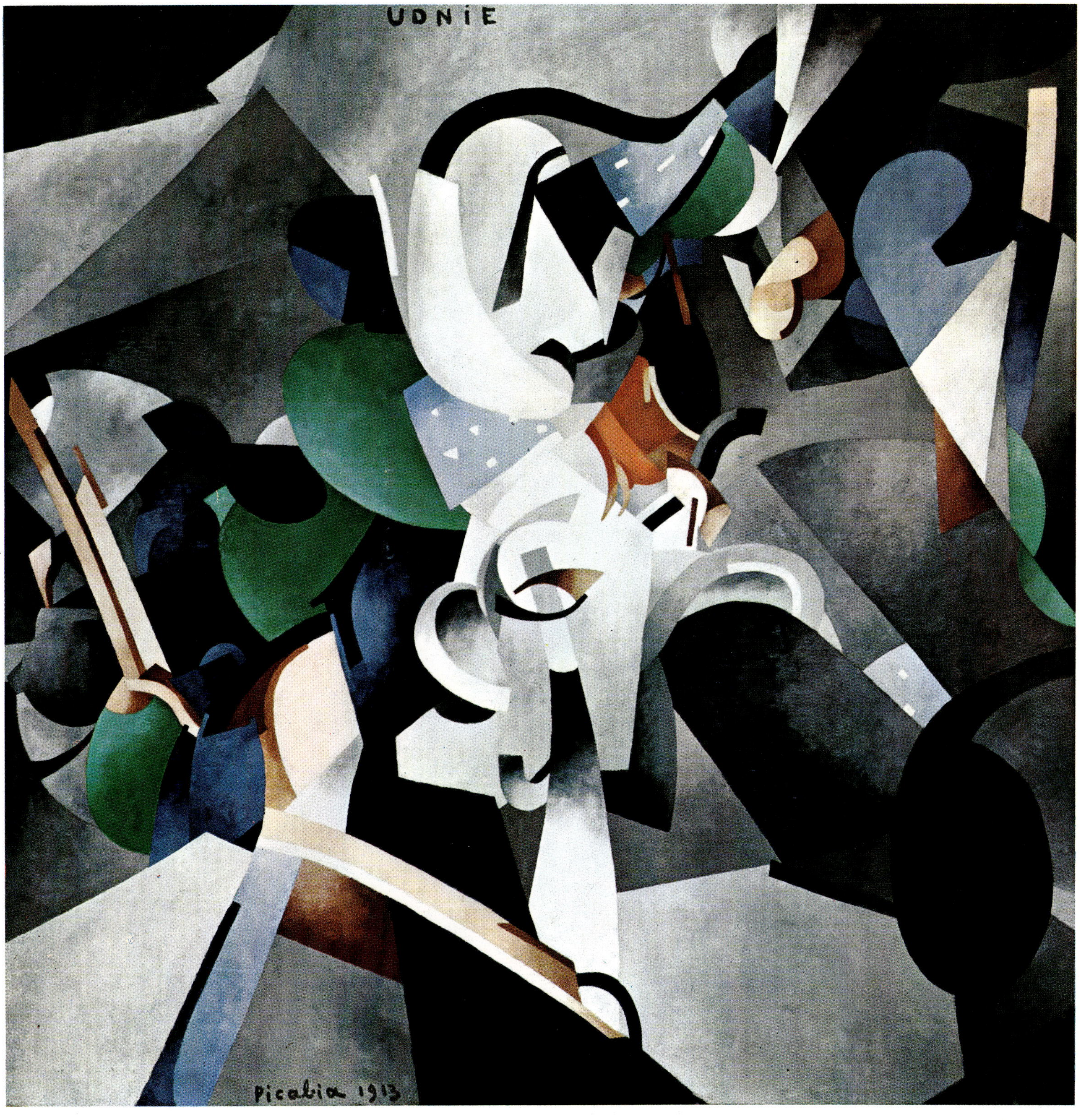

Francis Picabia: *Udnie,* 1913

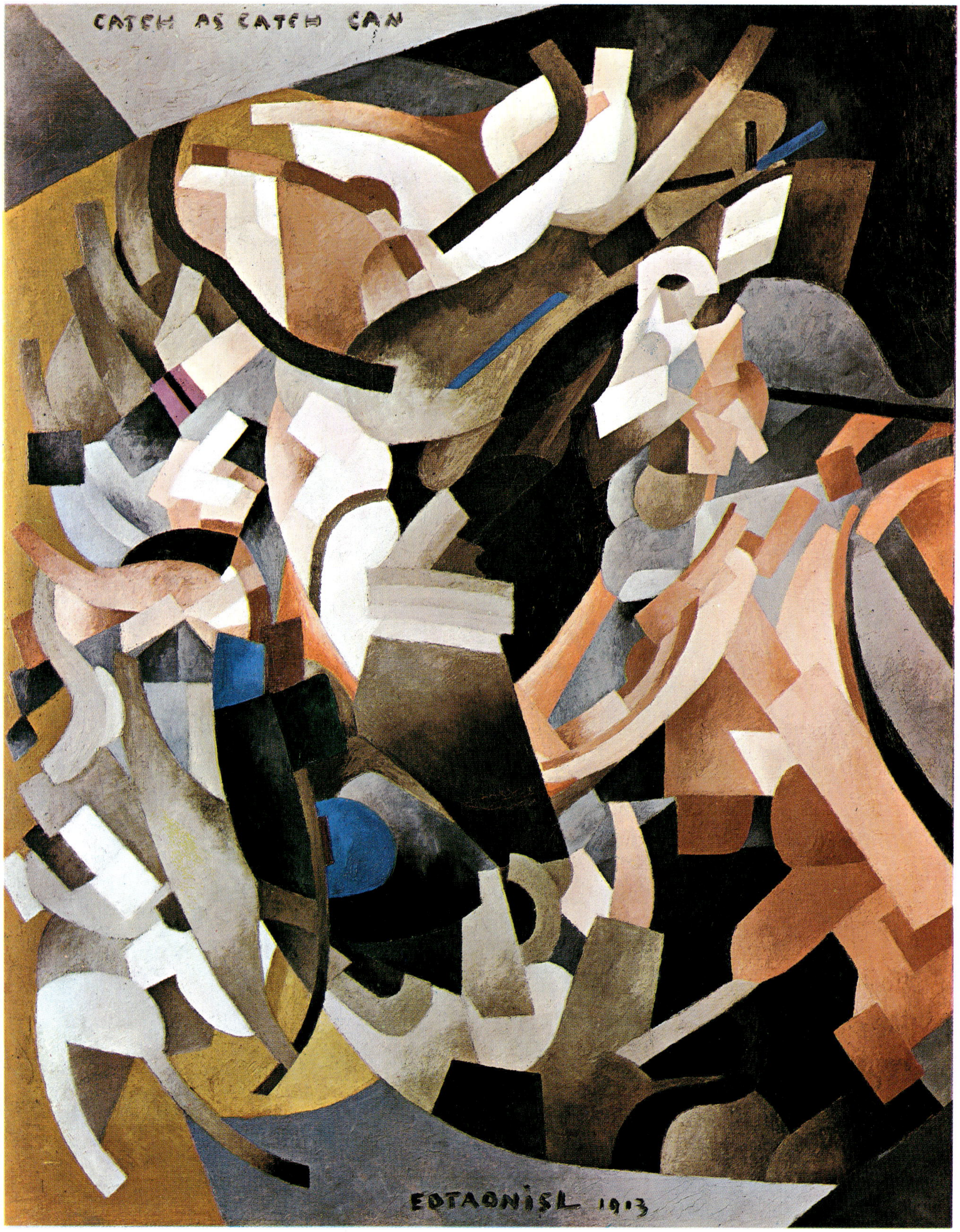

Francis Picabia: *Catch as Catch Can,* 1913